AIR CAMPAIGN

"BIG WEEK" 1944

Operation *Argument* and the breaking of the Jagdwaffe

DOUGLAS C. DILDY | ILLUSTRATED BY GRAHAM TURNER

OSPREY PUBLISHING
Bloomsbury Publishing Plc
Kemp House, Chawley Park, Cumnor Hill, Oxford OX2 9PH, UK
29 Earlsfort Terrace, Dublin 2, Ireland
1385 Broadway, 5th Floor, New York, NY 10018, USA
E-mail: info@ospreypublishing.com
www.ospreypublishing.com

OSPREY is a trademark of Osprey Publishing Ltd

First published in Great Britain in 2022

A catalogue record for this book is available from the British Library.

ISBN: PB 9781472824516; eBook: 9781472824523;
ePDF: 9781472824530; XML: 9781472824547

22 23 24 25 26 10 9 8 7 6 5 4 3 2 1
Maps by bounford.com
Diagrams by Adam Tooby
3D BEVs by Paul Kime
Index by Fionbar Lyons
Typeset by PDQ Digital Media Solutions, Bungay, UK
Printed and bound in India by Replika Press Private Ltd.

Photo on title page
Two 56th FG Thunderbolts taking off at RAF Halesworth in 1943. Highly experienced and well-led, "Zemke's Wolfpack" – named after its commander, Lieutenant Colonel Hubert "Hub" Zemke – was the highest-scoring Eighth AF fighter unit and its two combat groups were part of the 332 P-47s taking off to provide penetration support for the 1st and 2nd Bombardment Divisions' first mission in Operation *Argument*. (NMUSAF)

Author's Dedication
This book is dedicated to the loving memory of Sergeant Christopher Thomas Baker, 463 Squadron, RAAF, based at RAF Waddington, who lost his life during the very first mission of Operation *Argument* in the crash of Lancaster I DV338 call sign JO-C on the night of February 19/20, 1944.

Acknowledgement
I am deeply indebted to several people for their invaluable assistance in helping me, in one way or another, write this book. First and foremost, to my wonderful English friends Paul and Alison Crickmore. It was Paul who brought to my attention the comprehensive and detailed historical words of Stan D. Bishop and John A. Hey, *Losses of the US 8th and 9th Air Forces* (Bishop Book Productions, Yeovil, UK, 2007) that provided me with vital information that accurately determined the course of the daily battles of "Big Week". It was Alison's unflagging faith in and support for this project that resulted in this book being dedicated to her uncle, Chris Baker. In addition to Bishop and Hey's outstanding works, I was assisted by Donald Caldwell's equally excellent books, *Day Fighters in Defence of the Reich, A War Diary, 1942–45* and *The Luftwaffe over Germany, Defense of the Reich* (Frontline Books, Barnsley, UK, 2011 and 2014), that tell the story from the Luftwaffe side. For their outstanding assistance in the collection of photographs, I thank Ms Gina McNeely, who researched and obtained US National Archives and Records Administration (NARA) and German Bundesarchiv photos; Brett Stolle, who provided USAF images from the National Museum of the US Air Force (NMUSAF); and Sylvester Jackson, who obtained photos from the USAF Historical Research Agency (HRA). Finally, I am deeply indebted to Janet J. Capobianco for her ceaseless encouragement and support in completing this book. To all I give my sincere thanks and best wishes.

CONTENTS

INTRODUCTION

Military men of all nations agree that a determined air attack, once launched, is most difficult, if not impossible, to stop.

1st Lieutenant Kenneth N. Walker, ACTS Bombardment Aviation Instructor, Maxwell Field, Alabama, 1929–31

Boeing Model 299 at Seattle Tacoma factory, July 1935. (USAF Photo 060706-F-1234S-002)

The establishment of the US Army Air Forces' (USAAF) Eighth Air Force in January 1942 was the culmination of a decade-and-a-half-long crusade to prove that daylight precision bombing had a strategic war-winning capability. The quest formally began in July 1926 with the establishment of the Air Corps Tactical School (ACTS; originally the Air Service Field Officers School) at Langley Field, Virginia, home of the air arm's only bombardment group, the 2nd BG. Lack of proper permanent facilities and constant upheaval because of the creation of new units frequently interrupting the school's practical flying course caused the ACTS to be moved to a disused aviation repair depot at Maxwell Field, near Montgomery, Alabama, five years later.

Under Colonel John F. Curry, a World War I veteran aviator and American Expeditionary Force air service staff officer, at Maxwell the service's embryonic air power theory began to gestate in a setting completely detached from the practical realities of employment of bomber aircraft in a combat environment. Led by Curry's assistant commander, Major Walter Frank, the school's bomber proselytes began espousing the opinion that escorting fighters – which at the time lacked the range needed to accompany bombers on strategic attacks deep into enemy territory – were probably not necessary anyway. This remarkably naïve notion was so influential in the theoretical pontifications of the ACTS that by 1939 one instructor taught "we believe that a bombardment unit worth its salt is imbued with determination that it will penetrate any pursuit force in the world."

Fostered by Major Donald Wilson, an ACTS instructor from 1931–33, the school also began developing the idea that an air force sufficiently strong in long-range bombers could defeat an enemy nation by the destruction of the opponent's industrial fabric – the enemy's war-materiel-producing and distributing network composed of steel manufacturing, electrical power, and transportation systems. Since such specific targets could not be reliably located at night, the bombers would have to fly by day. Because fighters did not have the range to accompany the bombers, the latter would have to be so well armed that they would be self-defending.

To give substance to the theories being developed at the ACTS, in 1934 the Army Air Corps (USAAC, predecessor to the USAAF) issued a requirement (Circular Proposal [CP] 35-356) for a multi-engine bomber with a desired range of 2,000 miles and a speed of 250mph. The result was Boeing's Model 299, designated the XB-17 by the USAAC, and, at its roll-out on July 28, 1935, it was dubbed the "Flying Fortress" by a fawning press corps. It was an impressively large but elegantly designed, aerodynamically clean (streamlined all-metal airframe with flush riveting) aeroplane that averaged 252mph, flying non-stop the 2,280 miles from the Boeing factory airfield at Seattle, Washington, to Wright Field at Dayton, Ohio. Although the prototype was lost in a test flight crash due to crew error, the Flying Fortress immediately became the darling of air power advocates. While the crash influenced the War Department to order 133 Douglas B-18s (a DC-2 airliner redesigned as a bomber) as an interim substitute, at least Air Corps leadership had enough confidence in Boeing's design to order 13 YB-17s for service trials. The first example was flown to Langley Field and accepted by the 2nd BG on March 4, 1937.

Meanwhile, on March 1, 1935, in order to organize the USAAC's assorted combat units into a central command, Army Chief of Staff (COS) General Douglas MacArthur ordered the activation of General Headquarters Air Force (GHQAF). Naturally, the ACTS faculty was directed to provide the doctrine statement for the new air command: "The principal and all important mission of air power, when the equipment permits, is the attack of vital objectives in a[n enemy] nation's economic structure which will tend to paralyze that nation's ability to wage war."

GHQAF was regionally organized into four geographical districts (called Wings), each attached to one of the four field army headquarters (HQs) created two years prior. Commanding the 1st Wing (which included the 2nd BG at Langley) was Brigadier General Henry "Hap" Arnold, a strident bomber advocate and noted acolyte of the outspoken air power prophet Brigadier General William "Billy" Mitchell, Assistant Chief of the Air Service until his court-martial for insubordination in 1925. Ten years later, Arnold was appointed to become the Assistant Chief of Air Corps, where he was responsible for procurement and supply and enthusiastically promoted promising research and development projects, especially the revolutionary Flying Fortress and its intended successors, the B-24, B-29, and B-32.

Upon the death of USAAC chief Major General Oscar Westover in an air crash in September 1938, President Franklin Delano Roosevelt appointed Arnold as Chief of Air Corps, promoting him to major general. His new role was to oversee the enormous expansion of the USAAC to meet the rapidly increasing probability of having to fight another European conflict. To do so, he directed the reorganization of GHQAF's wings into four numbered air forces to command and control units within the Continental United States, and later created three more to defend the Philippines (Fifth AF), Panama Canal Zone (Sixth AF), and Hawaii (Seventh AF).

General Henry "Hap" Arnold, Chief of Staff, US Army Air Forces. (USAF Photo 021002-O-9999G-013)

Convinced that the USA would eventually be drawn into World War II, on July 9, 1941, President Roosevelt asked the War and Navy Departments for "estimates of production required to defeat our potential enemies." Arnold directed the Air Staff's newly created Air War Plans Department (AWPD) to provide the air power answer to defeating Germany. Supervised by Arnold's COS, Brigadier General Carl A. "Tooey" Spaatz, a specially selected team of four ACTS veterans – the core of the service's "bomber mafia" – convened and deliberated, essentially running an elaborate air campaign planning exercise complete with target lists, sortie requirements, damage expectations, and anticipated attrition rates. To provide a decisive strategic bombing offensive, the plan established that, by the spring of 1944, the USAAF would require 20 heavy bomber groups (960 B-17s and B-24s, with 400 spares) based in England and 12 very long range groups (576 B-29s and B-32s, with 240 spares) operating from Northern Ireland, along with ten fighter groups to defend the command's bases. Although known as AWPD/1, the resulting document went into the War Department's response to the President as "Annex 2: Munitions Requirements of the Army Air Forces to Defeat Our Potential Enemies" and was incorporated in the joint army-navy contingency plan Rainbow 5.

After Japan attacked Pearl Harbor and dramatically brought the USA into World War II, Arnold activated the Eighth AF on January 28, 1942, at Savannah, Georgia. It was soon given the mission of striking at the heart of the Third Reich from bases in the United Kingdom. At this point, the USAAF had the doctrine of high-altitude precision bombing of the enemy's industrial web, the aeroplane with which to implement it, and the plan with which to employ it against Nazi Germany. What it did not have was a long-range escort fighter to ensure that the bombers got through to their targets.

CHRONOLOGY

1941

June 20 US Army Air Forces (USAAF, formerly the USAAC) established as an autonomous military service administered by the army.

August 12 USAAF staff Air War Plans Division creates AWPD/1, the first planning document to address defeating Nazi Germany through the application of strategic air power.

December 7 Imperial Japanese Navy air strike on Pearl Harbor neutralizes US Pacific Fleet, resulting in US actively joining in World War II.

December 21 Arcadia Conference between Churchill and Roosevelt determines overall "Germany first" strategy and decides to build up US ground forces in Britain for a cross-Channel invasion of Nazi-occupied Europe in 1943 while USAAF and RAF implement a collaborative air offensive against German military power at its source.

1942

January 2 Eighth AF – the USAAF's first strategic air force – is activated at Savannah, Georgia. VIII Bomber and VIII Fighter Commands established as subordinate echelons 17 days later.

February 22 US/UK Combined Chiefs of Staff (CCS) publish "Policy for Disposition of US and British Air Forces", agreeing in principle for the RAF to continue night area bombing while the USAAF, once operational in UK, pursue daylight precision bombing.

June 25 Headquarters (HQ) Eighth Air Force arrived at Bushy Park, southwest of London.

August 17 First Eighth AF bomber mission flown against Nazi-occupied Europe.

September 6 USAAF staff produces AWPD-42 "Requirements for Air Ascendancy, 1942."

October Eighth AF ordered to begin bombing, as its primary mission, Kriegsmarine submarine pens at French ports in support of the upcoming Operation *Torch* and the Battle of the Atlantic. This lasts until June 1943.

November 8 Operation *Torch*, the Anglo-American invasion of French North Africa – substantial numbers of Eighth AF bomber and fighter groups transferred to support this peripheral ground campaign.

1943

January 14 Casablanca Conference between Churchill and Roosevelt prioritizes operations in Mediterranean over US build-up in UK and authorizes round the clock bombing of Germany.

January 21 CCS's Casablanca Directive implements UK/US strategic bombing accord.

January 27 First Eighth AF bomber mission against a target in Germany, Wilhelmshaven naval base, in support of anti-U-boat campaign.

June 10 CCS issues Directive for Operation *Pointblank*, formally launching the UK/US around the clock Combined Bomber Offensive (CBO), targeting a variety of German war materiel industries.

August 17 Eighth AF's increasingly ambitious series of deep penetration raids end with the first costly raid on Schweinfurt.

October 14 "Black Week" ends with Eighth AF's second disastrous raid on Schweinfurt, proving beyond doubt the critical need for long-range fighter escort.

October 15 I. Jagdkorps established by redesignating XII. Fliegerkorps, the Luftwaffe's night-fighter command, at Zeist, Netherlands; Generalleutnant Josef Schmid appointed commander.

First P-38 unit (55th FG) joins VIII Fighter Command for bomber escort duties.

November 1 Fifteenth AF – the second USAAF strategic air force – established in Tunisia, moving to Bari, Italy, one month later.

November 4 Operation *Argument* planning begins.

November 29 Operation *Argument* Directive passed to Eighth AF for individual mission planning.

December 5 First UK-based P-51B unit (354th FG/Ninth AF) becomes operational in the bomber escort role.

1944

January 6 Major General Carl A. Spaatz assumes command of US Strategic Air Forces in Europe and Lieutenant General James H. Doolittle appointed commander of Eighth AF.

January 27 Luftflotte Reich established by redesignating *Luftwaffebehlshaber Mitte* (Air Force Command, Centre); Generaloberst Hans-Jürgen Stumpff appointed commander.

February 11 Eighth AF's first P-51B escort unit (357th FG) becomes operational.

February 20 First mission of Operation *Argument*. Targets are aircraft factories at Leipzig, Bernburg, Braunschweig, Gotha, Halberstadt, Regensburg, and Tutow. Adverse weather precludes attacks on Regensburg and Tutow.

February 21 Eighth AF's second mission. Targets are aero-engine factories at Braunschweig, a major aircraft storage depot at Diepholz, and five airfields in northeastern Germany – adverse weather precludes most attacks.

February 22 Eighth AF's third mission. Targets are aircraft factories at Aschersleben, Bernberg, Gotha, Halberstadt, and Oschersleben – weather spoils almost all attacks. Fifteenth AF's second mission attacks the Regensburg Messerschmitt factories.

February 23 Fifteenth AF's third mission. Target is the Steyr anti-friction bearing factory.

February 24 Eighth AF's fourth mission. Targets are aircraft factories at Tutow and Gotha and the Schweinfurt ball-bearing industries. Fifteenth AF's fourth mission – target is the Steyr aircraft component factory.

February 25 Last missions of Operation *Argument*. Targets are aircraft factories at Regensburg, Augsburg, and Fürth and the anti-friction bearing factory at Stuttgart. Both Eighth and Fifteenth AFs attack the Regensburg Messerschmitt factories.

March 4 First Eighth AF attack on Berlin.

April 1 Operation *Pointblank* formally concluded – Eighth AF re-roled to support Operation *Overlord*.

June 6 D-Day – the successful Allied invasion of occupied France in Normandy.

ATTACKER'S CAPABILITIES

The spectacle of huge air forces meeting in [battle in] the air is the figment of imagination of the uninitiated.

Captain Harold L. George, ACTS Instructor, October 31, 1935

The *Pointblank* Directive

Republic P-47D-2-RE 42-8009 – an early Razorback Thunderbolt – on a test flight while assigned to the National Advisory Committee for Aeronautics (NACA, the forerunner of NASA) Glenn Research Center at Cleveland, Ohio. A big, robust, and powerful fighter, it was affectionately called "the Jug" because its rotund fuselage had the shape of a moonshine bottle. (NMUSAF 020930-O-9999G-013)

Initially commanded by now Major General Spaatz, in June 1942 the Eighth AF began moving to England, establishing itself in East Anglia with three bomber groups and 119 B-17Es. Because the Americans completely lacked combat experience, at the outset the command was essentially an on-the-job training organization. In fact, after a few raids to build experience, one bomb group (92nd BG) became a combat crew replacement training unit and did not fly operational missions until the next summer. Additionally, as soon as units were declared combat-ready, most were reassigned to the newly established Twelfth AF in September and October, destined to support the Allies' North African campaign, which began with Operation *Torch* on November 8.

To become General Dwight Eisenhower's European Theater of Operations Air Commander, Spaatz was transferred to North Africa in that same month. On 1 December, Brigadier General Ira C. Eaker, then in charge of VIII Bomber Command (VIII BC), was promoted to command the Eighth AF.

With the six B-17 bombardment groups remaining in England, Eaker was directed to mount a submarine pen campaign, attempting to destroy German U-boats in their steel-reinforced concrete bunkers at the French ports of Saint-Nazaire and Lorient, as well as Bordeaux, Brest, and La Pallice. This campaign lasted until June 1943. Consequently, the Eighth's first raid on targets in Germany did not occur until January 27, 1943, when 55 bombers attacked the port, shipyards, and naval base at Wilhelmshaven as part of the anti-U-boat campaign.

Meanwhile, following the Casablanca Conference (codename Symbol, January 14–24, 1943) between Churchill and Roosevelt, the USAAF and RAF were directed to begin around the clock bombing of Germany, with the objective being "the progressive destruction and dislocation of the German military, industrial, and economic system, and the undermining of the morale of the German people to a point where their capacity for armed resistance is fatally weakened."

The resulting Casablanca Directive implemented the agreement but provided only general, overarching guidance. More specific instructions were contained in the US/UK Combined Chiefs of Staff's amplifying Operation *Pointblank* Directive. This document was originally prepared by the USAAF headquarters' Committee of Operations Analysts (COA), a group

of strategic air campaign planners, each personally appointed by Arnold. In March 1943, the COA produced a report identifying "industrial targets in Germany the destruction of which would weaken the enemy most decisively in the shortest possible time." These were: aircraft and aero-engine manufacturing, anti-friction ball-bearing manufacturing, petroleum production, and U-boat construction. However, the COA "refrained from stating a formal order of priority for the target systems considered." Arnold was happy to allow the prioritization of operations for the destruction of these targets to be determined by USAAF field commanders.

When incorporated into the CCS's Operation *Pointblank* Directive, the RAF insisted that German fighter production be named a "first among equals." This determination has resulted in many historians mistakenly believing that *Pointblank* was directed against the Luftwaffe as the primary mission.

When the Eighth AF transferred to England in June 1942, it was commanded by Major General Carl A. Spaatz, with Brigadier General Ira C. Eaker commanding the subordinate VIII Bomber Command. When Spaatz was transferred to North Africa, Eaker took over as Eighth AF commander. (USAF Photo 021002-O-9999G-013)

But for USAAF field commanders, the COA's assessment that "The ball-bearing industry [42 percent of which was concentrated in Schweinfurt] appeared to offer the most economical and most operationally feasible method of impinging by air attack on the whole structure of German war production" proved to be too tempting a lure to ignore.

On May 18, after considerable discussion and debate, the CCS approved the Plan for the Combined Bomber Offensive from the United Kingdom, extracted the resulting guidance into a separate document, and issued it as the *Pointblank* Directive on June 10, leaving the details to be coordinated between Eighth AF and RAF Bomber Command. The stated objective was to weaken Germany militarily, industrially, and economically to the extent required "to permit initiation of final combined [ground] operations on the Contintent." This initially resulted in a balanced broad-based air campaign, not one concentrating on the destruction of the Luftwaffe.

Once the futile, frustrating, and unsuccessful submarine pen campaign was concluded and nine additional bomber groups had arrived in England, in the summer of 1943 the Eighth AF was finally able to start focusing on its primary mission, the piecemeal – but hopefully progressive – destruction of a variety of industries, which now included aluminum and synthetic rubber production, that were considered vital to Germany's war-making capabilities. Believing that Nazi cities were little more than "labour camps employed almost solely by the war effort," Air Chief Marshal (ACM) Sir Arthur "Bomber" Harris (head of RAF Bomber Command) was happy to continue killing civilians living near German industrial centers, making Operation *Pointblank* almost exclusively an American endeavor.

To do so, on June 6, 1943 – exactly one year before Operation *Overlord*, the Allies' famous D-Day invasion in Normandy – VIII BC had 13 bomber groups equipped with

Boeing B-17E/F Flying Fortresses and two more with Consolidated B-24D Liberators, some 720 bombers in total. Flying fighter sweeps over northern France and short-ranged escort missions – mostly for the command's three groups of B-26 medium bombers – VIII Fighter Command had four fighter groups equipped with 320 Republic P-47C/D Thunderbolts.

Aircraft: their capabilities, roles, and missions

Introduced in April 1942, the B-17F was a significant improvement over earlier models of the Flying Fortress. This model was defended by two pairs of Browning AN/M2 .50-cal machine guns in power-operated dorsal and ventral turrets and another pair in a tail-gunner position, plus five manually aimed Brownings.

The weak point in the Fortress's bristling defense was the front quarter, where there were two machine guns – one .50-cal, one .30-cal – for the bombardier and navigator to fire. Jagdwaffe (the Luftwaffe's single-engine fighter force) pilots quickly learned that, for survival and best effect, gutsy head-on attacks were preferred – Eighth AF losses to this tactic were shockingly high. This resulted in the B-17G mounting a powered Bendix chin turret with twin .50-cals for the bombardier to operate. Two .50-cal Brownings were also mounted in the cheek positions, but these were cumbersome and difficult for the navigator to aim and fire. Needless to say, these officers were not trained specifically as gunners and generally fired for morale effect.

The late B-17F-models and the B-17G had significantly increased fuel tankage (from 1,700 to 2,780 US gallons), giving them a one-way range of 2,900 miles (empty). These were generally issued to Major General Curtis Le May's 3rd Bombardment Division for the deeper penetration missions.

Powered by four Wright R-1820 Cyclone nine-cylinder radial engines, each with a Moss/ General Electric two-stage turbine-driven supercharger (or turbocharger), the Flying Fortress had a 182mph cruise speed with a 450–800 mile combat radius, depending on bombload. Its broad, exceptionally thick NACA 0018 wing could lift 8,000lb of bombs, or with a full fuel load it could haul 4,500lb of bombs to Berlin (600 miles).

The feature that made the B-17 an effective bombing platform was the relatively accurate Norden Mk XV (US Army designation M4) bombsight, permitting average USAAF bombardiers to place their ordnance within 400ft of an aimpoint from an altitude of 15,000ft. When dropping eight 500lb bombs – each with a lethal radius of 60–90ft, depending on the type of structure struck – this accuracy was sufficient for ensuring at least one hit.

Boeing B-17G-30-DL 42-38091 was a Douglas-built Flying Fortress that remained Stateside as a training machine assigned to 9th BG which flew for the USAAF School of Applied Tactics, based at Pinecastle Army Airfield (now McCoy AFB) near Orlando, Florida. (USAF HRA Photo)

For success, the Norden bombsight required clear weather for visually locating and releasing bombs on a specific target, conditions that proved much more rare than the American bomber advocates anticipated. Consequently, the RAF H2S "blind bombing" radar was adopted and improved into the AN/APS-15 (H2X) air-to-ground radar which was first employed by Eighth AF units in November 1943. The 482nd BG was established to test the new sophisticated apparatus, develop operational procedures, and train the command's bombardiers for employing the new device.

The Consolidated B-24D was also introduced in 1942, the product of Air Corps specification CP C-212-1, published three years previously, calling for a new four-engine heavy bomber to replace the B-17. The specification, which was written around Consolidated's independently developed Model 32 design proposal, required the new bomber to have double the B-17's bomb capacity (although the same weight bombload), a 3,000-mile range (1,200-mile combat radius), and 300mph-plus airspeed. Consolidated's designers took advantage of the new Davis wing, a high aspect ratio (glider-like) airfoil whose excellent lift-vs-drag coefficient provided increased fuel efficiency. This, plus the B-24's voluminous fuel tankage, resulted in greatly extended range with the same engine power.

The slab-sided fuselage, containing two tandem bomb bays, was suspended from the wing center-section (which incorporated a large integral fuel tank), and the resulting combination was a handful to fly, the glider-type wing causing the aircraft to wallow at cruise speed, making tight formation flying (needed for mutually supporting defensive fire) difficult, and requiring two huge vertical stabilizers and constant work by the pilots to keep it steady.

Powered by four turbocharged, twin-row, 14-cylinder 1,200hp Pratt & Whitney R-1830 Twin Wasp radial engines, it could haul 2,700lb of bombs for 1,200 miles, or more realistically, 5,000lb for 800 miles (or its full load of 8,000lb for 400 miles). While the more efficient wing allowed an operational cruise speed of 215mph, it could not fly as high as the B-17 when loaded, placing it within the lethal envelope of Luftwaffe heavy antiaircraft (AA) guns. Its greater range made it better suited for the Pacific, where distances were immense and there was less fighter and AA opposition, and for the North Africa/Mediterranean theaters, where German flak (contraction of *Fliegerabwehrkanone*, or aircraft defence cannon) weapons were primarily light/medium caliber with fewer of the dreaded 8.8cm batteries to contend with.

With either type, when the Eighth – and later the Fifteenth – AFs began prosecuting Operation *Pointblank* in earnest, fighter escort into the depths of the Third Reich was tragically absent. Fully committed to pursuing strategic bombing as a doctrine – and the means of assuring the Air Force's independence after the war – the Air Corps had deliberately neglected its development of fighter aircraft. Priority – meaning money and manpower – went to bombardment aviation, with improving fighter technology lagging badly behind. Despite being one of Billy Mitchell's protégés and leading the crusade for strategic bombing – and an independent Air Force – in November 1939, Hap Arnold suddenly and belatedly realized, following the Luftwaffe's shocking effectiveness in the Polish campaign, that "pursuit aviation – tactics and plane development – has not received the share of attention and interest in the Air Corps [that] it merits."

Much of this deliberate neglect was actually Arnold's own fault. To prevent the army from attempting to have the Air Corps develop or utilize its "pursuits" as army-support ground attack aircraft, Arnold ruled that – without exception – "pursuit aircraft [were] restricted to a maximum of 500lbs of armament, including ammunition." Additionally, in May 1939 he prohibited the development and use of external fuel (drop) tanks – proposed for the service's first-generation modern fighters (the Seversky P-35 and Curtiss P-36) – on the grounds that if the army knew these could carry drop tanks, then, logically, they could also carry bombs. Arnold feared this would open the door for the army to direct the development of what came to be called fighter-bombers, thereby siphoning off funding needed for the continued development of four-engine heavy bombers. He was so pedantic about these perceptions that he had the USAAF cling to the anachronistic pursuit name, banning the use of the more modern term "fighter" because it implied more general roles. Consequently,

Consolidated B-24D-7-CO Liberator 41-23828 was used as a training aircraft based at the USAAC four-engine pilot school located at Maxwell Field, near Montgomery, Alabama. Later, this Liberator was assigned to the 90th BG (321st Bomb Squadron) flying missions against Japanese targets in New Guinea and the Philippines. Nicknamed "Czech'em," it survived the war. (NMUSAF 040315-F-9999G-002)

Lockheed XP-38A – the twin-engine Lightning was initially developed as an "area defense interceptor" intended to be armed with a 37mm cannon, as well as four machine guns, to make it an effective bomber destroyer. Of the dozen YP-38s supplied to the 1st Pursuit Group for service trials, one (S/N 39-700) was modified with a cockpit pressurization system to become the sole XP-38A (40-762) in December 1942. (NMUSAF 020903-O-9999B-059)

when the Materiel Division's Engineering Section realized the need to mount heavy cannon on its pursuits in order to destroy large enemy bombers, the designs had to be termed "interceptors" in order to circumvent Arnold's arbitrary 500lb pursuit armament limitation.

Since the concept of escort fighters was largely abandoned as technologically infeasible, the USAAF's second generation – the promising Lockheed P-38 Lightning and pathetically disappointing Bell P-39 Airacobra – were specifically designed as area-defense and point-defense interceptors (stemming from CPs X-608 and X-609), respectively, each including a Colt T9 (army designation M4) 37mm autocannon. Meanwhile, the belated recognition that fighters capable of wresting air superiority over the battlefront would actually be needed, the USAAF's third pursuit generation became America's first multi-role fighters, despite what Arnold wanted them called. The P-35 morphed into the heavy but underpowered Republic (formerly Seversky) P-43 Lancer, while the P-36 became the P-40 Warhawk.

Of this evolutionary process, the Republic design was the clear winner. It stemmed directly from the June 1939 Air Corps Board prioritization report that – as Priority #3 – called for "a fighter to rank with the best in the world." Specifically, it was intended that the type – which at that time looked to be the Lancer's successor, the P-44 Rocket – be superior to the RAF Spitfire and the Luftwaffe's Messerschmitt Me 109. But when the first combat reports from the Battle of Britain – including the RAF's evaluation of a captured Messerschmitt Me 109E – arrived, the Materiel Division realized that the P-44 would be "obsolete by the time the first one flew, let alone reached production," so it was cancelled before the first prototype was built.

Fortunately, Republic's aeronautical engineers had already conceived of how to wrap a far more powerful fighter around Pratt & Whitney's new, and massive, 2,500hp two-row 18-cylinder R-2800 Double Wasp turbocharged radial engine. First flown in May 1941, the P-47 epitomized American fighter design philosophy – bigger is better – overcoming substantial weight and drag with enormous power. Burning specially formulated 100-octane aviation fuel (avgas), with 2,535hp driving a four-blade, 12ft diameter paddle-bladed propeller, at 25,000ft the Thunderbolt's maximum speed was 430mph, 30mph faster than the Luftwaffe's Me 109G (which had a 1,455hp 12-cylinder engine using 87-octane fuel to turn a three-bladed 9ft 10in diameter prop) and 20mph faster than the newer Focke-Wulf Fw 190A. Armed with eight .50-cal Brownings, its weight of fire was markedly superior to both German types. With a 11,936lb combat weight and a commensurately high wing loading, it lacked the maneuverability to beat either in a turning fight, but it could out-climb them above 20,000ft and out-dive anything with wings, allowing the pilot to disengage at will.

A true, robust multi-role fighter, it could carry two 1,000lb bombs from underwing shackles that were plumbed for drop tanks. Originally, the P-47D had a 230-mile combat radius, but with progressively larger drop tanks, by 1944 it could range 475 miles, all the way to Hamburg and Frankfurt from its East Anglia airfields. Marginally superior in all regards except maneuverability, when flown by the men graduating from the USAAF's superior pilot training program, the "Jug" (so-called because of its rotund fuselage) soon proved dominant over the Luftwaffe's fighters when flying in the bomber escort role.

The real game changer, however, was the North American Aviation (NAA) P-51 Mustang. Originally conceived as a P-40 substitute to augment the Spitfire in the RAF, NAA's brainchild benefited from the new NACA 45-100 laminar flow wing – a highly efficient, symmetrical, high-speed airfoil where the maximum thickness was well aft, maintaining boundary layer control and minimizing induced drag – and conical lofting fuselage design, where the smoothly tapered airframe effectively enclosed all drag-producing components, such as the radiator and oil cooler. Powered by the P-40's 12-cylinder 1,150hp Allison V-1710, the NA-73 design attained 382mph at 15,000ft (30mph faster than the P-40 and Spitfire Mk V). But while the engine's single-speed, single-stage gear-driven (mechanical) supercharger boosted performance at lower altitudes, power diminished rapidly as altitude increased.

In May 1940, the British Purchasing Commission ordered 320 (later 620) Mustang Mk Is, two of which were provided to the Air Corps for testing as XP-51s. Concurrently, the service's June 1940 Air Corps Board met to reset priorities for technological development. Still not cognizant of combat realities, the need for an "escort fighter with a 1,500-mile range" (to accompany the B-24) was listed as Priority #4. Confronted with the looming possibility of actually going to war, the service's political agenda (independence from the army) was now trumped by operational necessities and Arnold swapped the escort fighter with Priority #1, the very long range heavy bomber (B-29 and B-32). At the time, how this previously determined infeasible requirement was to be met was anybody's guess.

Meanwhile, the RAF decided to improve the Mustang's higher altitude performance by installing the 1,565hp Rolls Royce Merlin 61 engine, which had a new two-speed, two-stage mechanical supercharger, the test machine flying in October 1942. Because the XP-51s performed best at low altitude, in June that year, under CP X-630, the Air Corps ordered 1,200 P-51As as ground attack fighters (i.e., fighter-bombers), capable of carrying two 500lb bombs or a pair of 75 or 150 US gallon drop tanks. Six weeks after the RAF, the USAAF also installed the Merlin 61 in two P-51As, the new engine having just entered license production as the supercharged 1,520hp Packard V-1650. Based on engineering data alone, the service had cancelled the bulk of the P-51A order, replacing it with an order for 2,200 P-51B/Cs (the identical P-51C being produced in NAA's second factory). Carrying six .50-cal Brownings, the redesigned Mustang's top speed was 440mph, but more importantly, with half the fuel consumption rate, the P-51B/C could range 475 miles on internal fuel alone, as far as a P-47 could with drop tanks.

In the final phase of his epiphany, in February 1942, Arnold ordered "all-out development of [jettisonable, external] auxiliary fuel tanks for the P-51, P-38, and P-47." However, the Materiel Division's design for the 200gal steel ferry tank was over-engineered and its testing unduly extensive, the protracted delay prompting Arnold, in June 1943, to give USAAF "a fighter [apparently Arnold had gotten over his reluctance to use this word] that can protect our bombers… Get to work on this right away because by January '44, I want a fighter escort for all our bombers from the U.K. into Germany." As an expedient, VIII Fighter Command approved the purchase of British-made 108gal pressed cardboard tanks on 1 July. However, the devoted disciples of the self-defending bomber at Eighth AF HQ did not place the first order until early October, following the command's bloody nose over Schweinfurt.

But because the P-51A was typecast as a ground support fighter (even to the extent that it spawned the A-36 Apache

North American Aviation XP-51 41-039, one of two provided from the RAF's initial order of Mustang Is, assigned for flight testing to the NACA Research Facility at Langley, Virginia. The outstanding fighter of World War II, it took the USAAF months to realize that it had a game changer in its inventory that would eventually enable the defeat of the Luftwaffe in 1944. (NMUSAF 061023-F-1234P-005)

dedicated ground attack aircraft), and to simplify maintenance and repair, the Merlin-powered P-51B/C was initially relegated to USAAF fighter groups headed to England to join the reorganized Ninth AF, which was being transferred from North Africa to England to support the ground offensive once Operation *Overlord* put Allied troops on French soil. The first of these was the 354th FG (Fighter Group), the Pioneer Mustang Group, but at last the need for the Mustang as an escort fighter had been realized and, shortly after the next unit – the 357th FG – arrived, it was transferred to the Eighth AF in exchange for the P-47-equipped 358th FG.

The Air Staff finally recognized the Mustang's potential as a long-range escort fighter in July 1943 through Colonel Mervin Gross – Assistant COS for Materiel, Maintenance, and Distribution – whose report comparing all available fighter types selected the P-51 as most suitable for the role. Consequently, the 357th's Stateside training was extended so that, in October 1943, its squadrons could conduct familiarization flying with bombers for a month. Leaving its P-39D fighter-trainers behind, the group moved to New York for embarkation on RMS *Queen Elizabeth*. Issued brand-new P-51Bs upon arrival in England, with the new drop tanks the group could fly combat missions of 650 (beyond Berlin with US-built 75gal tanks) to 850 miles (beyond Vienna with British-made 108gal tanks), completely changing the complexion of the air war against the Third Reich.

Commanders

Commanding all American heavy bomber forces in Europe was Lieutenant General Carl A. "Tooey" Spaatz. Born in 1892 to a German immigrant family named Spatz (he changed the spelling to Spaatz, pronounced "spots", in 1937 to seem more Dutch than Deutsche), he graduated from the army's Military Academy at West Point in 1914 to become one of the air service's 26 original pilots. Advancing rapidly with the World War I expansion, Spaatz commanded the 31st Aero Squadron, a training unit flying Nieuport pursuit planes, and was placed in charge of the 3rd Aviation Instruction Center at Issoudun in France. To get combat experience, he briefly flew SPAD XIIIs with the 13th Aero Squadron, being credited with shooting down two German fighters.

Between the wars, Spaatz commanded a pursuit group, a bombardment group, and a bomber wing; attended the ACTS; and became the new air staff's first Chief of Plans until Arnold made him his COS. Subsequently, Spaatz commanded Eighth AF for seven months before being transferred to North Africa in November 1942. Following the Casablanca Conference and the amalgamation of Allied air commands, he was appointed commander of the Northwest Africa Air Command in February 1943.

Sardonic, taciturn, and reticent, Spaatz was known as a man of few words who – by delegating nettlesome details to subordinates – could get the job done. RAF Chief of Air Staff ACM John Slessor wrote that he was "a man of action rather than speech, with an uncommon flair for the really important issue and a passionate faith in the mission of air power." Very much a realist unbound by ACTS doctrine, having directed large forces that suffered significant losses attacking German and Italian targets, Spaatz was a believer in the need for fighter escort.

Once the North African and Sicilian campaigns were successfully concluded, and after the newly established Fifteenth AF joined Operation *Pointblank*, in January 1944 Spaatz was appointed to command the US Strategic Air Forces in Europe (initially USSAFE, later USSTAF) to oversee all American strategic bombing operations. His assignment – as ordered by Arnold – was specifically to lead the air campaign to attain air superiority over northern France for the cross-Channel invasion scheduled that summer.

Accompanying Spaatz to England was Major General James H. "Jimmy" Doolittle, who had commanded the Northwest Africa Strategic Air Force (NASAF) for nine months.

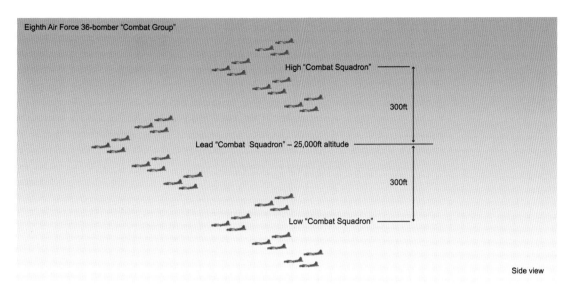

Eighth Air Force 36-bomber "Combat Group"

High "Combat Squadron"

300ft

Lead "Combat Squadron" – 25,000ft altitude

300ft

Low "Combat Squadron"

Side view

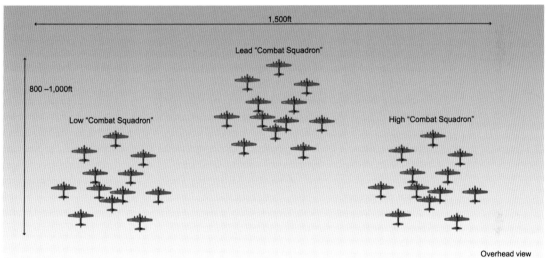

1,500ft

Lead "Combat Squadron"

800 –1,000ft

Low "Combat Squadron"

High "Combat Squadron"

Overhead view

ABOVE EIGHTH AIR FORCE COMBAT WING FORMATIONS

During the second half of 1943, Luftwaffe rocket-firing interceptors forced the Eighth AF to spread their formations wide trying to minimize the effectiveness of these BR 21 rocket attacks. This change resulted in the use of a mile-wide vertically stacked 54-plane "combat box"(usually two or more bomb groups) formation that was used during the hard-fought battles of August and October 1943.

In December, the advent of effective fighter escorts – where P-47Ds started destroying large numbers of slower, less manoeuvrable twin-engine Me 110Gs – had largely neutralized the rocket attacks to the point where VIII Bomber Command could begin concentrating their formations into the much more compact 1,500ft-wide "combat groups", each composed of 36 bombers (usually one bomb group). Two "combat groups" – the second following the first with four miles spacing – formed a "combat wing" with the trailing formation bombing the same target independently of the first.

The new formation provided a much greater concentration of bomb impacts, which was especially important when dropping was based on radar-equipped "pathfinder" blind-bombing missions. For visual bombing, having the second "combat group" follow in-trail closely behind the "combat wing" leader allowed the second formation to make last-minute adjustments upon seeing the impacts of the first group's bombs, resulting in greater accuracy. Additionally, the more compact "combat groups" – using less than one-third the airspace occupied by the previous year's "combat box" formations – were much easier to protect by escorting fighters.

OPPOSITE EIGHTH AIR FORCE BOMBER UNITS AND BASES, FEBRUARY 1944

Doolittle was a celebrated pilot during aviation's golden age and was America's reigning air hero, having been awarded the Medal of Honor for leading a squadron of B-25s – taking off from a US Navy aircraft carrier – on a morale-boosting bombing raid against Japan in April 1942. Born in California in 1896, he joined the Air Service during World War I and spent the war as an instructor at Rockwell Field, near San Diego. An aeronautical genius as well as a gifted pilot, Doolittle was awarded the first-ever doctorate degree in aeronautical engineering from Massachusetts Institute of Technology the same year he won the Schneider Cup (1925, flying a Curtiss R3C-2 racing floatplane). Four years later, he won the Harmon Trophy for pioneering instrument ("blind") flight equipment, procedures, and flying techniques.

Resigning his commission to fly for the Shell Oil Company in 1930, Doolittle fostered the firm's development of 100-octane avgas for high performance aircraft engines, while winning the Bendix Trophy (1931) and Thompson Trophy (1932) and setting a new world speed record (296mph) in the Shell Speed Dash (also 1932). With the advent of World War II initiating the USAAC's ambitious expansion, Doolittle returned to active service as a troubleshooter at various aircraft factories and was an advisor on Arnold's staff before the chief selected him to lead Special Project No. 1, the raid on Tokyo that bears his name. Promoted to brigadier general as a result of his sensationalized success, he was sent to England to command Eighth AF's 4th Bombardment Wing, flying B-26 medium bombers.

In September 1942, when Operation *Torch* was conceived and Twelfth AF was established as its American air component, Arnold appointed Doolittle as commander, promoting him to major general two months later. In the post-Casablanca reorganization, he was put in charge of the NASAF, directing four heavy bomber, five medium bomber, and four fighter groups (all from Twelfth AF) and RAF No. 242 Group (ten Vickers Wellington night bomber squadrons). Because US law directed that legal authority for matters of discipline, promotion, assignment, and other functions be administered through the formal command structure, Spaatz assumed command of Twelfth AF, freeing Doolittle to concentrate on directing combat operations in the Sicily campaign and the invasion of Italy.

Short, stocky, and balding, Doolittle was a natural leader as well as a fast learner. He was known as being compassionate and considerate, determined, yet flexible. As the USAAF's

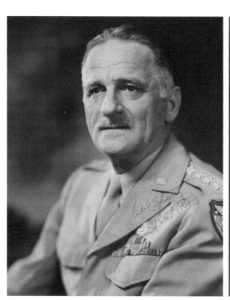

RIGHT
General Carl A. "Tooey" Spaatz. (USAF HRA Photo)

FAR RIGHT
Lieutenant General James H. "Jimmy" Doolittle. (NMUSAF 020903-o-9999b-097)

RAF Horsham St Faiths
96th Combat Bomb Wing
458th Bomb Group

RAF Seething
448th Bomb Group

RAF Bungay
446th Bomb Group

Norwich

Kettering Hall
HQ 2nd Bombardment Division

RAF Hethel
2nd Combat Bomb Wing
389th Bomb Group

RAF Tibenham
445th Bomb

RAF Thorpe Abbots
100th Bomb Group

RAF Horham
13th Combat Bomb Wing
95th Bomb Group

RAF Framlingham
390th Bomb Group

Lowestoft

RAF Old Buckenham
453rd Bomb Group

RAF Wendling
392nd Bomb Group

RAF Shipdham
14th Combat Bomb Wing
44th Bomb Group

RAF Deopham Green
452nd Bomb Group

RAF Snetterton Heath
45th Combat Bomb Wing
96th Bomb Group

RAF Knettishall
388th Bomb Group

RAF Honington HQ
3rd Bombardment Division

Bury St Edmunds
HQ 4th Combat Bomb Wing

RAF Great Ashfield
385th Bomb Group

RAF Rattlesden
447th Bomb Group

Ipswich

RAF Ridgewell
381st Bomb Group

RAF Earls Colne
94th Bomb Group

Colchester

Peterborough

RAF Polebrook
94th Combat Bomb Wing
351st Bomb Group

RAF Glatton
457th Bomb Group

RAF Molesworth
41st Combat Bomb Wing
303rd Bomb Group

RAF Kimbolton
379th Bomb Group

RAF Deenethorpe
401st Bomb Group

RAF Grafton Underwood
384th Bomb Group

RAF Chelveston
305th Bomb Group

RAF Podington
92nd Bomb Group

RAF Thurleigh
40th Combat Bomb Wing
306th Bomb Group

Bedford

Cambridge

RAF Hardwick
20th Combat Bomb Wing
93rd Bomb Group

RAF Bassingbourn
1st Bombardment Division and
1st Combat Bomb Wing
91st Bomb Group

Luton

Northampton

London

Bushy Hall
VIII Fighter Command HQ

Bushy Park
USSTAF HQ

High Wycombe
Eighth AF HQ

USAAF Headquarters

Eighth AF Bombardment Division HQs
and Combat Bomb Wing HQs

B-17 bases

B-24 bases

N

0   10km
0   10 miles

Major General William E. "Bill" Kepner in the cockpit of a Republic P-47 Thunderbolt. (USAF HRA Photo)

highest ranking reserve officer, he was not wedded to the service's self-defending bomber dogma, and as early as May 1943 he determined that long-range fighter escort was key to the success of bomber operations. Writing to Arnold, he stated that fighter escort was "desirable in the past … [but] essential in the future" and that it was now "critical" because newer, up-gunned Luftwaffe fighters' armament outranged the bombers' .50-cal machine guns.

With the surrender of Italy (announced on September 8, 1943) and the Allied invasion at Salerno (Operation *Avalanche*) the next day, another reorganization of Mediterranean air commands was undertaken the following month, Arnold taking the opportunity to establish a second strategic bomber force – Fifteenth AF – based in Italy on November 1, putting Doolittle in command. Initially provided with six heavy bomber, three medium bomber, and four fighter groups (931 aircraft), Doolittle began striking Combined Bomber Offensive (CBO) targets in Austria and Bavaria as well as supporting the torturous Allied ground advance up the Italian peninsula. When Arnold decided to organize the USSAFE under Spaatz to coordinate and direct both the Eighth and Fifteenth AFs, he also decided it was time for a leadership change in the former, and appointed Doolittle to take over the UK-based command. Doolittle turned Fifteenth AF over to Major General Nathan A. Twining, who had successfully led Thirteenth AF in the Pacific theater's Solomon Islands campaign, and headed north to England. Doolittle took command of Eighth AF on January 6, 1944.

Heading Doolittle's VIII Fighter Command was Major General William E. "Bill" Kepner, who had replaced Hunter in August 1943. Born in 1893 in rural Indiana, Kepner fought – and was wounded – in World War I as an infantry officer and afterwards transferred to the Air Service as a balloon and airship pilot, participating in numerous test projects and record-breaking flights. His interest in expanding the envelope of lighter-than-air (LTA) flight led to his appointment to head the Materiel Division's LTA branch. After learning to fly aeroplanes in 1931, he returned to the division as Chief of Purchasing.

Another talented aviator with an engaging mind and scientific intellect, Kepner continued participating in record-setting events, attended the ACTS in 1936, and afterwards became commander of the 8th Pursuit Group at Langley Field. As the USAAC expansion developed, Kepner advanced through key air defense and army support (ground attack) commands to lead IV Fighter Command, then Fourth AF, headquartered at San Francisco.

Because of his practical, scientific approach and broad experience in aircraft development and fighter employment – as well as being based near the major US aviation manufacturers in California – Arnold assigned him the task of finding a solution to American fighter range limitations. Kepner spearheaded and directed the industry's efforts to increase internal fuel tankage in the P-38 and P-51 and to quickly field workable drop tanks, thus bypassing the slow, tedious, and protracted Materiel Division testing processes. His success made him Arnold's choice for replacing Hunter.

A confirmed bachelor and a true "pilot's general," Kepner ate, drank, and frequently flew with his men, completing 24 combat missions during the war. Courteous and compassionate, he was also completely dedicated to defeating Germany. Unaffected by ACTS teaching – being an LTA pilot during the bomber advocates' crusades of the 1920s made him immune to the associated controversies – Kepner was determined to rid Western European skies of Luftwaffe fighters. He knew they would be swarming around the Eighth AF's bombers, so he strove relentlessly to place as many fighters as possible in their immediate vicinity and accompany them all the way to their targets and back.

ORDERS OF BATTLE, FEBRUARY 1944

US Strategic Air Forces in Europe
Lieutenant General Carl A. Spaatz — HQ: Bushy Park
USAAF Eighth Air Force
Major General James H. Doolittle — HQ: High Wycombe
1st Bombardment Division
Major General Robert B. Williams — HQ: RAF Bassingbourn

1st Combat Bombardment Wing		**RAF Bassingbourn**
91st Bomb Group	Boeing B-17F/G	RAF Bassingbourn
381st Bomb Group	Boeing B-17F/G	RAF Ridgewell
40th Combat Bombardment Wing		**RAF Thurleigh**
92nd Bomb Group	Boeing B-17F/G	RAF Podington
305th Bomb Group	Boeing B-17F/G	RAF Chelveston
306th Bomb Group	Boeing B-17F/G	RAF Thurleigh
41st Combat Bombardment Wing		**RAF Molesworth**
303rd Bomb Group	Boeing B-17F/G	RAF Molesworth
379th Bomb Group	Boeing B-17F/G	RAF Kimbolton
384th Bomb Group	Boeing B-17F/G	RAF Grafton Underwood
94th Combat Bombardment Wing		**RAF Polebrook**
351st Bomb Group	Boeing B-17G	RAF Polebrook
401st Bomb Group	Boeing B-17G	RAF Deenethorpe
457th Bomb Group	Boeing B-17G	RAF Glatton

2nd Bombardment Division
Major General James P. Hodges — HQ: Kettering Hall

2nd Combat Bombardment Wing		**RAF Hethel**
389th Bomb Group	Consolidated B-24D/H	RAF Hethel
445th Bomb Group	Consolidated B-24H/J	RAF Tibenham
453rd Bomb Group	Consolidated B-24H/J	RAF Old Buckenham
14th Combat Bombardment Wing		**RAF Shipdham**
44th Bomb Group	Consolidated B-24H/J	RAF Shipdham
392nd Bomb Group	Consolidated B-24H/J	RAF Wendling
491st Bomb Group	Consolidated B-24H/J	(not yet operational)
20th Combat Bombardment Wing		**RAF Hardwick**
93rd Bomb Group	Consolidated B-24H/J	RAF Hardwick
446th Bomb Group	Consolidated B-24H/J	RAF Bungay
448th Bomb Group	Consolidated B-24H/J	RAF Seething

3rd Bombardment Division
Major General Curtis E. LeMay — HQ: RAF Honington

4th Combat Bombardment Wing		Bury St Edmunds
94th Bomb Group	Boeing B-17F/G	RAF Earls Colne
385th Bomb Group	Boeing B-17F/G	RAF Great Ashfield
447th Bomb Group	Boeing B-17G	RAF Rattlesden
13th Combat Bombardment Wing		**RAF Horham**
95th Bomb Group	Boeing B-17F/G	RAF Horham
100th Bomb Group	Boeing B-17F/G	RAF Thorpe Abbots
390th Bomb Group	Boeing B-17F/G	RAF Framlingham
45th Combat Bombardment Wing		**RAF Snetterton Heath**
96th Bomb Group	Boeing B-17F/G	RAF Snetterton Heath
388th Bomb Group	Boeing B-17F/G	RAF Knettishall
452nd Bomb Group	Boeing B-17G	RAF Deopham Green

VIII Fighter Command
Major General William E. Kepner — **HQ: Bushey Hall**

65th Fighter Wing — Saffron Walden

4th Fighter Group	Republic P-47D/NAA P-51B	RAF Debden
56th Fighter Group	Republic P-47D	RAF Halesworth
355th Fighter Group	Republic P-47D	RAF Steeple Morden
356th Fighter Group	Republic P-47D	RAF Martlesham Heath

66th Fighter Wing — Sawston Hall

55th Fighter Group	Lockheed P-38H	RAF Nuthampstead
78th Fighter Group	Republic P-47D	RAF Duxford
353rd Fighter Group	Republic P-47D	RAF Metfield
357th Fighter Group	North American P-51B	RAF Leiston
361st Fighter Group	Republic P-47D	RAF Bottisham

67th Fighter Wing — Wolcot Hall

20th Fighter Group	Lockheed P-38J	RAF Kings Cliffe
352nd Fighter Group	Republic P-47D	RAF Bodney
359th Fighter Group	Republic P-47D	RAF East Wretham

USAAF Fifteenth Air Force
Major General Nathan A. Twining — **HQ: Bari, Italy**

5th Bombardment Wing — Foggia, Italy

2nd Bomb Group	Boeing B-17F	Amendola, Italy
97th Bomb Group	Boeing B-17F	Amendola, Italy
99th Bomb Group	Boeing B-17F	Tortorella, Italy
301st Bomb Group	Boeing B-17F	Lucera, Italy

47th Bombardment Wing — Manduria, Italy

98th Bomb Group	Consolidated B-24H	Lecce, Italy
376th Bomb Group	Consolidated B-24H	San Pancrazio, Italy
449th Bomb Group	Consolidated B-24H	Grottaglie, Italy
450th Bomb Group	Consolidated B-24H	Manduria, Italy
451st Bomb Group	Consolidated B-24H	Gioia del Colle, Italy

304th Bombardment Wing — Cerignola, Italy

454th Bomb Group	Consolidated B-24H	San Giovani, Italy
455th Bomb Group	Consolidated B-24H	San Giovani, Italy
456th Bomb Group	Consolidated B-24H	Stornara, Italy
459th Bomb Group	Consolidated B-24H	(not yet operational)

306th Fighter Wing — Foggia, Italy

1st Fighter Group	Lockheed P-38H	Salsola, Italy
14th Fighter Group	Lockheed P-38J	Triolo, Italy
82nd Fighter Group	Lockheed P-38J	Vincenzo, Italy
325th Fighter Group	Republic P-47D	Foggia, Italy

Oberkommando der Luftwaffe
Reichsmarschall Hermann Göring
Luftflotte Reich – Generaloberst Hans-Jürgen Stumpff — **HQ: Berlin-Wannsee**
I. Jagdkorps – Generalmajor Josef Schmid — **HQ: Zeist, the Netherlands**
1. Jagddivision – Oberst Günther Lützow — **HQ: Döberitz (near Berlin)**

Unit	Base	Strength/Aircraft
III./JG 54	Ludwigslust	19 Me 109G-6
ZG 26 I. Gruppe	Völkenrode	29 Me 110G-2
II. Gruppe (-)	Hildesheim	21 Me 410A/B
NJG 2 I. Gruppe	Kassel-Rothwesten	21 Ju 88C-6
II. Gruppe	Parchim	17 Ju 88C-6

NJG 5	Stab	Döberitz	4 Me 110G-4
	I. Gruppe	Stendal	18 Me 110G-4
	II. Gruppe	Parchim	21 Me 110G-4
	III. Gruppe	Neuruppin	15 Me 110F/G
	IV. Gruppe	Brandis	16 Me 110G-4

2. Jagddivision – Generalmajor Max-Josef Ibel — HQ: Stade (near Hamburg)

JG 11	Stab	Husum	7 Me 109G-5
	I. Gruppe	Husum	52 Fw 190A-6/-7
	II. Gruppe	Wunstorf	46 Me 109G-5/-6
	III. Gruppe	Oldenburg	32 Fw 190A-5/-6
			11 Me 109G-6
	10. Staffel	Aalborg, Denmark	11 Fw 190A-5
	11. Staffel	Lister, Norway	19 Bf 109T-2
II./JG 3		Rotenburg an der Wümme	43 Me 109G-6
ZG 26	Stab	Wunstorf	3 Me 110G-2
	III. Gruppe	Wunstorf	27 Me 110G-2
NJG 3	Stab	Stade	2 Me 110G-4
	I. Gruppe	Vechta	18 Me 110G-4
	II. Gruppe	Schleswig	16 Ju 88C-6
	III. Gruppe	Stade	20 Me 110G-4
	IV. Gruppe	Westerland	17 Ju 88C-6
II./NJG 4		Fassberg	19 Do 217N

3. Jagddivision – Generalmajor Walter Grabmann — HQ: Deelen, the Netherlands

JG 1	Stab	Deelen	4 Fw 190A-6
	I. Gruppe	Rheine	23 Fw 190A-7
	Sturmstaffel 1	Rheine	12 Fw 190A-7/R2
	II. Gruppe	Rheine	18 Fw 190A-6
	III. Gruppe	Volkel	49 Me 109G-6
JG 3	I. Gruppe	Mönchen-Gladbach	32 Me 109G-6/U4
	IV. Gruppe	Venlo	38 Me 109G-6
NJG 1	Stab	Bönninghardt	3 Me 110G-4
	I. Gruppe	Venlo	8 Me 110G-4
			9 He 219A-0
	II. Gruppe	St Trond	13 Me 110G-4
	III. Gruppe	Twente	17 Me 110G-4
	IV. Gruppe	Leeuwarden	21 Me 110G-4
NJG 2	Stab	Deelen-Arnhem	2 Ju 88C-6
	III. Gruppe	Gilze-Rijen/Venlo	27 Ju 88C-6/R2

7. Jagddivision – Generalleutnant Joachim-Friedrich Huth — HQ: Schleissheim (Munich)

JG 3	Stab	Neubiberg	5 Me 109G-6
	III. Gruppe	Leipheim	42 Me 109G-5/-6
I./JG 5		Regensburg-Obertraubling	36 Me 109G-6
II./JG 27		Wiesbaden-Erbenheim	17 Me 109G-6
5./ZG 26		Oberpfaffenhofen	10 Me 410B-1/U4
ZG 76	Stab	Ansbach	4 Me 110G-2
	I. Gruppe	Ansbach	28 Me 110G-2
	II. Gruppe	Neubiberg	39 Me 110G-2
NJG 6	Stab	Schleissheim	3 Me 110G-2
	I. Gruppe	Mainz-Finthen	25 Me 110G-4
	II. Gruppe	Stuttgart-Echterdingen	27 Me 110G-4

NJG 101	Stab	Ingolstadt-Manching	3 Me 110G-2
	I. Gruppe	Ingolstadt-Manching	3 Me 110E/G
			3 Ju 88C-6
	II. Gruppe (-)	Munich-Riem	19 Do 217N
	III. Gruppe	Kitzingen	32 Me 110C/D/E/F/G
NJG 102	Stab	Kitzingen	3 Me 110G-4
	I. Gruppe	Kitzingen	13 Me 110F/G
	II. Gruppe	Stuttgart	13 Me 110E/F/G

Jagdfliegerführer Ostmark
(subordinated to 7. Jagddivision)

		Vienna-Cobenzl	
I./JG 27		Fels-am-Wagram	52 Me 109G-6
II./JG 53		Vienna-Seyring	37 Me 109G-6
II./ZG 1		Wels	38 Me 110G-2
6./NJG 101		Parndorf	9 Do 217N

30. Jagddivision (Wild Sau)
Oberst Hans-Joachim Herrmann   **HQ: Berlin**

JG 300	Stab	Deelen	3 Fw 190A-5
	I. Gruppe	Bonn-Hangelar/Jüterbog	16 Me 109G-5/-6
	II. Gruppe	Rheine (Atchd to 3.JDiv)	6 Fw 190A-5
	III. Gruppe	Wiesbaden-Erbenheim	1 Me 109G-6
JG 301	Stab	Schleissheim	2 Me 109G-6
	I. Gruppe	Neubiberg	16 Me 109G-5/-6
	II. Gruppe	Vienna-Seyring	3 Me 109G-6
	III. Gruppe	Zerbst	30 Me 109G-6
JG 302	Stab	Döberitz	4 Me 109G-6
	I. Gruppe	Jüterborg-Waldlager	14 Me 109G-6
	II. Gruppe	Ludwigslust	3 Fw 190A-5/U8
	III. Gruppe	Oldenburg	Shared III./JG 11 aircraft
I./KG 7 'Beleuter' ('Illuminator')		Münster-Handorf	41 Ju 88A-4

Luftflotte 3
Generalfeldmarschall Hugo Sperrle   **HQ: Paris, France**
II. Jagdkorps – Generalleutnant Werner Junck   **HQ: Chantilly, France**
4. Jagddivision – Oberst Carl Vieck   **HQ: Metz, France**

JG 26	Stab	Lille-Nord	2 Fw 190A-5/-6
	I. Gruppe	Florennes, Belgium	34 Fw 190A-5/-6/-7
	II. Gruppe	Cambrai-Epinoy	38 Fw 190A-5/-6/-7
	III. Gruppe	Dinant, Belgium	35 Me 109G-3/-6
NJG 4	Stab	Chenay	2 Me 110E-2/G-4
	I. Gruppe	Florennes, Belgium	11 Me 110D/F/G
5 Ju 88C-6			
	II. Gruppe	St. Dizier/Dijon	5 Me 110F-4/G-4
			19 Do 217N

5. Jagddivision
Generalmajor Karl Hentschel   **HQ: Paris, France**

JG 2	Stab	Cormeilles-en-Vexin	7 Fw 190A-7/R6
			2 Me 109G-6
	II. Gruppe	Creil	49 Me 109G-6
	III. Gruppe	Cormeilles-en-Vexin	29 Fw 190A-5/-6/-7
III./ZG 1		Bordeaux-Merignac	Unkn Ju 88Cs

DEFENDER'S CAPABILITIES

If our theorists had had knowledge of radar in 1935, the American doctrine of strategic bombing in deep daylight penetrations would surely not have evolved.

Major Haywood S. Hansen, ACTS Instructor, 1935–38,
Commander of Eighth AF's 1st Bombardment Wing, 1942–43

The Luftwaffe's air defense system

Like the USAAF, the Luftwaffe was also an aggressively minded, highly offensive force, though focused on tactical air support of the army rather than at the strategic level. Defence against enemy bombers was initially entrusted to the Flakartillerie branch which spread its AA batteries across ten local air defense districts (*Luftgauen*) and established a sparse 20-mile-wide belt of flak guns behind the Westwall, the thin line of scattered fortifications from the Eifel region to the Swiss border. Lacking an air defense network, these units were originally semi-autonomous until the Luftwaffebehlshaber Mitte (Air Force Command, Centre), under Generaloberst Hubert Weise, was organized in March 1941 to coordinate the ground-based defenses against the increasingly bothersome RAF Bomber Command's night bombing campaign.

As Bomber Command's indiscriminate nocturnal operations became increasingly serious, five months later the Luftwaffe was forced to organize a radar-based, radio-controlled fighter defense system, operated by XII. Fliegerkorps, a dedicated night-fighter command. Led by General der Flieger Josef Kammhuber, Germany's air defense command was directly subordinate to Reichsmarschall Hermann Göring's *Reichsluftfahrtministerium* (RLM, or Reich Aviation Ministry) and consisted of five *Nachtjagdgruppen* (night-fighter groups), two searchlight divisions, and three signals regiments.

The Messerschmitt Me 109 had been the Luftwaffe's standard light fighter for the first four years of the war and remained the most numerous. With the uprated DB 605A engine and upgunned with additional underwing-mounted MG 131s, the Gustav model was an effective bomber destroyer but lacked the performance and maneuverability to match newer American fighters. (Bundesarchiv, Bild 101I-487-3066-04, Fotograf(in): Boyer)

Piggy-backing on the night air defense system, the next year the growing threat posed by the Eighth AF's increasing daylight bombing operations prompted the formation of three *Jagddivisionen* (fighter divisions) covering Germany, a fourth in Austria three months later, and eventually two more in occupied France. By the end of 1943, the Luftwaffe's six fighter divisions mustered five Jagdgeschwadern and two Zerstörergeschwadern, comprising 18 single-engine day fighter groups equipped with Me 109s and Fw 190s, and six Zerstörergruppen flying Me 110/410 twin-engine destroyers. They also contained six twin-engine Nachtjagdgeschwadern, consisting of 20 night-fighter groups – augmented by two under-strength training wings and a seventh, autonomous Jagddivision containing nine single-engine Wild Sau (wild boar) night-fighter groups.

Additionally, each fighter division covering Germany also had four *Luftnachrichten Regiments* (air communications regiments), with the divisions based in Austria and France having two or three. Each regiment was assigned to a sector's fighter-control station (*Jägerleit Stellung* or *Jagdabschnittstellung*) and contained three battalions. The *Flugmeldedienst* (aircraft warning service) battalion operated the early warning (EW), search, and tracking radars. The *Flugwachtdienst* (aircraft observer service) battalion visually tracked aircraft formations, filling gaps in radar coverage caused by terrain and Allied jamming. Finally, the *Jägerleit abteilung* (fighter-control battalion) was composed of situation and operations room plotting, ground control intercept (GCI), and technical repair companies.

To provide centralized control of the Reich's now round the clock air defense effort, on September 15, 1943 the night-fighter XII. Fliegerkorps was redesignated *I. Jagdkorps* (fighter corps), with Generalmajor Josef Schmid appointed as its commander. I. Jagdkorps was the main and central component of the *Reichsverteidigung* (Defence of the Reich) integrated air defense system (IADS).

This robust and rapidly developing system included an expansive coastal EW radar network composed of 32 FuMG 80 Freya and 57 FuMG 62A Würzburg radars stretching from Brittany to Denmark. With a range of 120 miles, the 125MHz/20kW Freya air search radar could detect British and American bomber formations assembling over southeast England, while the shorter-range (18 miles) 560MHz/8kW Würzburg target tracking radar provided reasonably accurate altitude data as the raiders approached the coast.

These were supplemented by several large, powerful FuMo 51 Mammut (*Mammoth*), which used eight Freya-type antennae mounted together and its 200kW power to detect targets as far out as 180 miles, and the tall FuMG 41 and 42 Wasserman (*Aquarius*), which used four or eight (depending on the version) Freya-type antennae stacked vertically and could "see" 120 miles along a very narrow, rotatable azimuth, improving bearing resolution. The EW radars were augmented by the Luftwaffe's separate *Funkaufklärungsdienst* (signals intelligence service), which monitored RAF and USAAF radio traffic and gave a heads up when increased activity signaled that a major raid was being launched.

The Flugmeldedienst's interior radar array was known as the Kammhuber Line and was composed of a string of radar sites, spaced about 20 miles apart, forming a line from the tip of Jutland, through

The Luftwaffe FuMG 42 Wassermann Schwere (heavy) early warning radar consisted of eight Freya antenna arrays mounted vertically on a massive 60-meter (197ft) tall, 4-meter (13ft) diameter steel pipe mast. Broadcasting on 120–150MHz using 100kW power, the Wassermann S had a maximum effective range of 180 miles for targets at and above 20,000ft, but a lesser range for lower altitudes. (Steve Zaloga)

northwest Germany, Holland, and Belgium, then curving through eastern France back to the Swiss border. Each site was equipped with one Freya search radar and two Giant Würzburg tracking radars, one for tracking the incoming bombers, the other for locating intercepting fighter formations by tracking the leader's (*Leitjäger*) FuG 25 Erstling (first-born) IFF transponder. The data from each site was passed directly to the sector's fighter-control station (*Jägerleit Stellung* or *Jagdabschnittstellung*), where it was combined with that from their own radars (two each of EW, Freyas and Giant Würzburgs) to create a *Luftlage* (air situation).

Initially, for intercepting RAF night bombers, at each Jägerleit Stellung, the *Jägerleitoffizier* (JLO or fighter-control officer, the sector's GCI controller) used the Flugmeldedienst's target and interceptor tracking information to vector night-fighters using close control – providing headings and target range, bearing and altitude information – to place the interceptor within visual or on-board radar range of the targets. However, the Allies' use of chaff (bundles of thin metal foil strips, called Window) and electronic jamming (codenamed Carpet) largely neutralized the Giant Würzburg tracking radars, making close control practically impossible in near-chaotic combat situations.

This forced I. Jagdkorps to revert to broadcast control, whereby the targets' general locations (using map grid-squares), direction of travel, and altitude were provided along with approximate heading and the map grid-square in which the bomber formations could expect to be intercepted. For this purpose, the Jägerleit Stellung staff plotted the radar returns of the incoming bomber formations and used information from its FuSAn 733 Y-*Bodenstelle* (ground station) – the main component of the *Y-Verfahren-kampf* (Y-Battle Control) system – to create a Luftlage report which was continuously updated and transmitted to the Jagddivision's *Jägerleit Zentral Gefechtsstand* (Fighter-control Battle Centre).

From the division's component Jägerleit Stellungen, its own co-located radar site (three EWs and two each of Freyas and Giant Würzburgs), and visual tracking information from the *Flugwachtkommandos* (FluKo, aircraft observer reporting centers), the HQ Jägerleit staff would to create an overall air situation picture (*Luftlagebild*). The collated radar, observer, and signals intelligence information was then projected onto a special vertical 30-by-40ft screen called the *Hauptlage Karte* (main situation map).

The 3. Jagdivision "battle opera house" operations room and command center at Deelen, Holland, where incoming raids, as well as the locations of defending fighters and flak units, were projected on the large vertical board to the right (#5/6/7/2) called "the main situation map". This information came from the enemy raid tracking section (#4) and the friendly fighter situation group (#8), and was projected by the signals technicians (#3). The battle commander (#1) organized the defensive responses to the incoming raids through orders to the fighter-direction officers (*Jägerleitoffiziere*) sitting in the four rows of desks in front of him. (US Army)

OPPOSITE LUFTFLOTTE REICH IADS SYSTEM DIAGRAM

Luftflotte Reich's IADS was a robust and technically sophisticated command and control network that attempted to correlate and communicate a number of information streams. Incoming raids were first detected by long-range EW radars positioned along the North Sea coastline, and their information was forwarded directly to the Jagddivision and Jagdkorps HQs.

Once the raid penetrated into Luftflotte Reich airspace, a broad band of target and fighter tracking radar sites picked up the raids and passed their tracking data to the *Jägerleit Stellung* (Fighter-control Station), which forwarded this information to the *Jägerleit Zentral Gefechtsstand* (Fighter-control Battle Centre) at the Jagddivision HQ. Additionally, beginning in February 1944, the *Flugwacht Kommandostellung* (FluKo Stations), which collected the *Flugwachtdienst* (Air Watch Service) observation posts' reports of visually tracked enemy bomber formations, began passing their information to to the Jagddivision's Battle Centre instead of the local *Luftgauen* (air defence district) HQ.

Using the correlated target and fighter tracking information, the Jagddivision Battle Centre – 3. Jagddivision's radio callsign was "Diogenes" – directed its interceptor forces to engage the incoming Eighth AF bomber formations using broadcast control radioed to the leaders of airborne fighter units. Additionally, "Diogenes" forwarded the air situation picture *(Luftlagebild)* to *Seeäuber* (Pirate), the I. Jagdkorps HQ, which coordinated the responses of the RVL's other Jagddivisions and passed the Luftlagebild to Luftflotte Reich HQ in Berlin, which broadcast it as the Reichsjägerwelle, a continuous running commentary to interceptor units not yet engaged in the day's air battle.

From this big picture display, the Jagddivision commander or his operations officer – the *Jagdfliegerführer* (JaFü or fighter director, the division's GCI controller) – would direct the division's JLOs to scramble interceptor units, control the interceptions by airborne units, or pass orders to the appropriate sector controller(s) to do so.

The division HQ also forwarded the information to I. Jagdkorps HQ, which broadcast a running commentary (*Reichsjägerwelle*) on the raids' locations, directions, and altitudes, keeping all fighter formations awaiting scramble orders and those airborne not being actively vectored on intercepts, as well as augmenting fighter training flights and factory defense units, informed of the location and direction of the developing American air attacks.

Aircraft: their capabilities, roles, and missions

The fighter component of the German IADS was known as the *Reichluftverteidigung* (RLV, or Aerial Defense of the Reich). Four years into World War II, the Luftwaffe's standard fighter plane was still the Messerschmitt 109, its designation now prefixed with "Me" rather than the original "Bf" for *Bayerische Flugzeugwerke* (Bavarian Aircraft Factory). Upgraded with progressive horsepower increases, the Gustav model was powered by the 1,475hp Daimler Benz DB 605A 12-cylinder in-line engine. The DB 605A had a hydraulically positioned variable speed mechanical supercharger that automatically compensated for air pressure changes, providing excellent power output at all altitudes and a top speed of 398mph at 20,996ft.

The Focke Wulf Fw 190 was the Luftwaffe's third generation fighter and was intended to replace the Me 109. An excellent air-to-air fighter initially, significant teething troubles delayed large-scale deployment, with most going to the Eastern Front where the type's inherent ground-attack capabilities proved badly needed. Upgunned and heavily armored, the type also lacked the performance and maneuverability to match newer American fighters. (NMUSAF 050602-F-1234P-005)

Normally mounting two Rheinmetall-Borsig 13mm MG 131 machine guns and a Mauser 20mm MG 151/20 autocannon in the nose, its armament was considered inadequate for destroying an American bomber on one pass unless its pilot's marksmanship and determination to get close to his target were uncommonly high. Consequently, many of I. Jagdkorps' 366 Me 109G-5/G-6s were also armed with another pair of MG 131s, each mounted in an underwing gondola, giving the sub-variant the nickname *Kanonenboot* (gunboat). An additional 32 G-6s (I./JG 3) had the U4 modification, replacing the MK 151/20 with the much heavier and harder-hitting Rheinmetall-Borsig MK 108 30mm cannon. Additionally, some

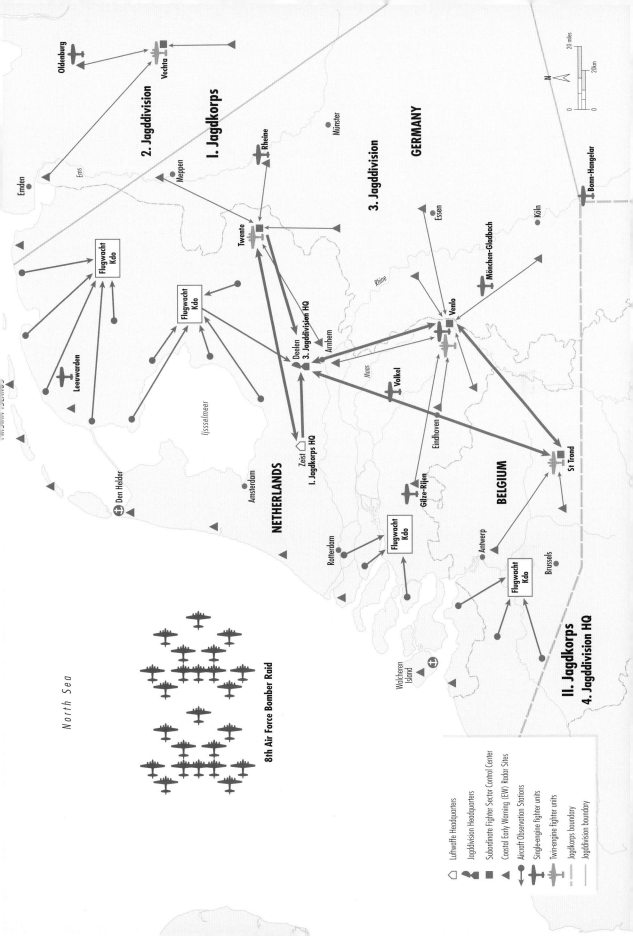

North Sea

8th Air Force Bomber Raid

Oldenburg

Vechta

2. Jagddivision

I. Jagdkorps

Emden

Ems

Meppen

Rheine

Münster

GERMANY

Twente

3. Jagddivision

Essen

Köln

Mönchen-Gladbach

Bonn-Hangelar

Flugwacht Kdo

Flugwacht Kdo

Leeuwarden

Deelen

3. Jagddivision HQ

Arnhem

Rhine

Venlo

Den Helder

Ijsselmeer

Amsterdam

Zeist

I. Jagdkorps HQ

NETHERLANDS

Maas

Volkel

Eindhoven

Gilze-Rijen

St Trond

BELGIUM

Rotterdam

Flugwacht Kdo

Antwerp

Brussels

Flugwacht Kdo

Walcheren Island

II. Jagdkorps

4. Jagddivision HQ

N

20 miles

20km

0

0

Luftwaffe Headquarters

Jagddivision Headquarters

Subordinate Fighter Sector Control Center

Coastal Early Warning (EW) Radar Sites

Aircraft Observation Stations

Single-engine fighter units

Twin-engine fighter units

Jagdkorps boundary

Jagddivision boundary

OPPOSITE LUFTFLOTTE REICH FIGHTER UNITS AND BASES, MID-FEBRUARY 1944

Gustavs were also modified with two underwing Bordrakete 21s (BR 21, on-board rockets), an aerial adaptation of the army's 21cm Nebelwerfer 42 infantry barrage rocket, the 131lb projectile having an effective range of 3,900ft and a lethal blast radius of almost 50ft. Two of these and their underwing launching tubes added another 494lb to the aircraft, significantly degrading its flying performance.

At 6,940lb fully loaded, the Me 109G-6 was a lightweight amongst its contemporaries, but the ever-increasing armament, armor, and equipment upgrades were accommodated at the expense of maneuverability, climb rate, and other performance factors. Appreciably slower – by 30–40mph – than American single-engine fighters, and unable to outmaneuver them above 20,000ft or escape by diving away, "109" pilots generally avoided engaging P-47s and P-51s if at all possible.

Augmenting the nearly 400 Me 109Gs were 129 Focke-Wulf Fw 190A Würger (*Shrikes*), the Luftwaffe's third-generation light fighter, originally intended to replace the Me 109. Much heavier (at 10,870lb loaded) than its predecessor, the Fw 190A-3 and later versions were powered by the mechanically supercharged 1,677hp BMW 801D-2 two-row, 14-cylinder radial engine, giving it a top speed of 408mph at 19,420ft. Excelling in performance and maneuverability at low and medium altitudes, the aircraft's simple, single-speed supercharger's augmentation diminished markedly above 20,000ft, making it 20–30mph slower than American fighters at altitudes where the bombers flew. Indeed, the power loss was so dramatic that, fully loaded, the type's maximum operational altitude was 24,935ft, barely high enough to engage the higher-flying American bomber formations.

The A-6 was the most common variant, armed with a pair of small 7.92mm MG 17 light machine guns in the upper cowling and four 20mm MG 151/20E cannon in the wings, and, especially when carrying a pair of BR 21 air-to-air rocket tubes, proved to be another powerful bomber destroyer. However, because of its reduced performance at the higher altitudes, the heavy interceptor was vulnerable to escorting fighter attacks, so typically a formation of Fw 190s would be covered by a *Höhenstaffel* (high squadron) of lighter Me 109Gs.

The I. Jagdkorps' second-line bomber interceptors were the 59 twin-engine Me 110Gs and 31 examples of its intended replacement, the Me 410 second-generation Zerstörer heavy fighter. Originally designed and intended to be a long-range bomber escort, the former lacked the maneuverability to contend with enemy single-engine interceptors – especially against RAF Hurricanes and Spitfires in the Battle of Britain – and the *Zerstörerwaffe* (destroyer force) was decimated by the end of that campaign and was virtually disbanded shortly thereafter.

The survivors were relegated primarily to night-fighter, fighter-bomber and reconnaissance roles, but three years later the Eighth AF's increasingly strong and persistent daylight bombing

The Messerschmitt Me 110G was an uprated version of the Bf 110C/D that proved to be an epic failure during the Battle of Britain. Its standard four 7.92mm MG 17 and two MG 151/20 cannon nose armament was augmented with a belly pack containing a pair of MK 108 30mm cannon and an under-wing quartet of BK 21 air-to-air rocket tubes, making it very effective at breaking up the combat boxes of USAAF heavy bombers during autumn 1943. (NMUSAF 050602-F-1234P-011)

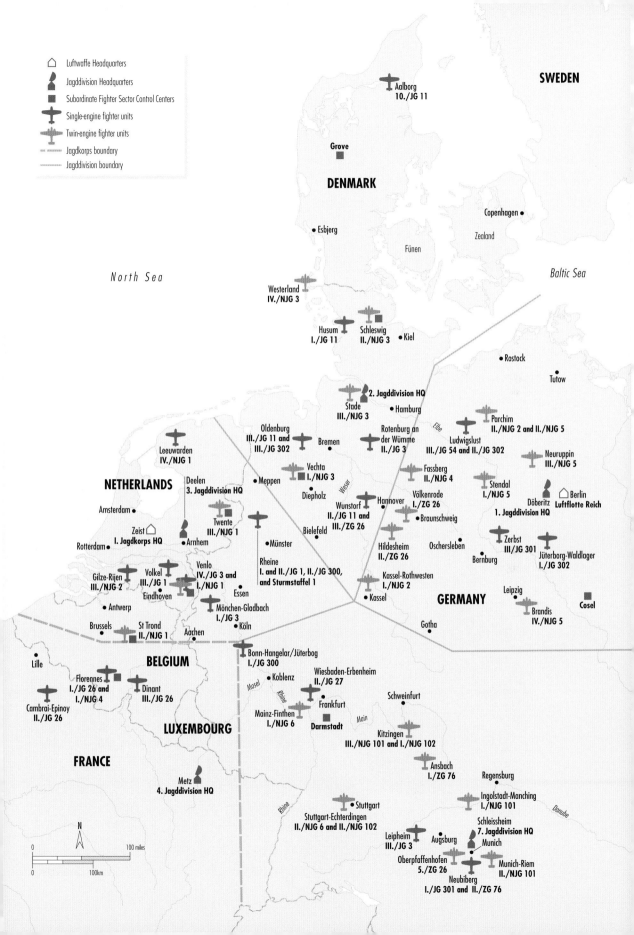

SWEDEN

North Sea

Baltic Sea

DENMARK

Aalborg
10./JG 11

Grove

• Esbjerg

Copenhagen •

Fünen

Zealand

• Kiel

Westerland
IV./NJG 3

Husum
I./JG 11

Schleswig
II./NJG 3

• Rostock

Tutow

NETHERLANDS

Leeuwarden
IV./NJG 1

Deelen
3. Jagddivision HQ

Amsterdam •

Zeist
I. Jagdkorps HQ

Arnhem •

Rotterdam •

Gilze-Rijen
III./NJG 2

Volkel
III./JG 1

Eindhoven •

Venlo
IV./JG 3 and
I./NJG 1

Essen •

Mönchen-Gladbach
I./JG 3

• Antwerp

Brussels •

St Trond
II./NJG 1

Aachen •

BELGIUM

Florennes
I./JG 26 and
I./NJG 4

Dinant
III./JG 26

Cambrai-Epinoy
II./JG 26

• Lille

LUXEMBOURG

FRANCE

Metz
4. Jagddivision HQ

Oldenburg
III./JG 11 and
III./JG 302

• Bremen

Vechta
I./NJG 3

• Meppen

Diepholz •

Wunstorf
II./JG 11 and
III./ZG 26

Rheine
I. and II./JG 1, II./JG 300,
and Sturmstaffel 1

• Münster

Bielefeld •

Stade
III./NJG 3

2. Jagddivision HQ

• Hamburg

Rotenburg an
der Wümme
II./JG 3

Fassberg
II./NJG 4

Hannover •

Völkenrode
I./ZG 26

• Braunschweig

Hildesheim
II./ZG 26

Kassel-Rothwesten
I./NJG 2

• Kassel

• Oschersleben

Parchim
II./NJG 2 and II./NJG 5

Ludwigslust
III./JG 54 and II./JG 302

Neuruppin
III./NJG 5

Stendal
I./NJG 5

Döberitz

Berlin
Luftflotte Reich

1. Jagddivision HQ

Zerbst
III./JG 301

Bernburg •

Jüterborg-Waldlager
I./JG 302

GERMANY

Leipzig •

Brandis
IV./NJG 5

Cosel

Gotha •

Bonn-Hangelar/Jüterbog
I./JG 300

Koblenz •

Wiesbaden-Erbenheim
II./JG 27

Mosel

Rhine

Mainz-Finthen
I./NJG 6

Frankfurt

Darmstadt

Main

• Schweinfurt

Kitzingen
III./NJG 101 and I./NJG 102

Ansbach
I./ZG 76

Regensburg •

Stuttgart-Echterdingen
II./NJG 6 and II./NJG 102

• Stuttgart

Rhine

Ingolstadt-Manching
I./NJG 101

Leipheim
III./JG 3

Oberpfaffenhofen
5./ZG 26

Neubiberg
I./JG 301 and II./ZG 76

Augsburg •

Munich •

Schleissheim
7. Jagddivision HQ

Munich-Riem
II./NJG 101

Danube

Legend:
- Luftwaffe Headquarters
- Jagddivision Headquarters
- Subordinate Fighter Sector Control Centers
- Single-engine fighter units
- Twin-engine fighter units
- Jagdkorps boundary
- Jagddivision boundary

N

0 — 100 miles
0 — 100km

raids on the Reich led to a resurrection of the Zerstörerwaffe, with three Gruppen (becoming the reconstituted ZG 26) being withdrawn from Russia and Italy to northern Germany and a fourth (II./ZG 1) moving to Austria. The latter was joined by two new Gruppen – the reconstituted ZG 76 – which was formed primarily from Me 110 reconnaissance units.

The obsolescent Me 110G's new role was as a Pulk-Zerstörer (*Pulk* was the traditional German cavalry term for regiment and slang for the large formations of USAAF bombers). Mounting a pair of MG 151/20 20mm and two MK 108 30mm cannons, and lugging four BR 21 air-to-air rocket tubes, the lumbering twin-engine destroyers could remain out of range of the American .50-cal machine guns and lob rockets into their tight, mutually supporting combat boxes, breaking up the formations so that intercepting single-engine fighters could engage more effectively. The Messerschmitt's cannon armament outranged the Flying Fortresses' and Liberators' machine guns, allowing the Zerstörers to get some kills of their own – at least until American escorting fighters arrived on the scene.

One Zerstörergruppe (II./ZG 26) was reequipped with the newer, but just as hapless, Me 410A/B Hornisse *(Hornet)*. A redesign of the fatally flawed Me 210, the Hornisse was more powerful and faster, but also heavier, which made it even less maneuverable than its predecessor. The A-model was intended to be a fast light bomber, equipped with a bomb bay beneath the cockpit, but being more urgently needed as a Pulk-Zerstörer, the bomb bay was converted to mount additional air-to-air weapons. The A-1/U2 modification mounted a total of four MG 151/20 cannon. One squadron had its Me 410s modified as A-1/U4s to mount the Rheinmetall BK 5 50mm cannon (derived from the army's half-track-mounted KwK39 L/60) instead of the second pair of MG 151/20s.

Finally, for point defense of cities, bases, and vital industrial centers, Göring and the Luftwaffe leadership initially placed great faith in their AA artillery arm. This publicly visible – and emotionally reassuring – spectacle of the Nazi Party's protection of the German population contained half of the Luftwaffe's personnel and consumed 29 percent of the regime's weapons budget and 20 percent of its munitions in 1943. By February 1944, the Luftwaffe had 1,402 heavy flak-gun batteries (8,412 guns) stationed within greater Germany, 70 percent of them being equipped with the famous high-velocity 8.8cm-Flak 41 and its earlier versions, the rest being the 10.5cm-Flak 38/39 and 12.8cm-Flak 40. The "dreaded 88" had an effective operational ceiling of 26,240ft, although accuracy diminished markedly above 20,000ft. Consequently, it could barely reach B-17 formations, usually flying at 23,000–25,000ft, but was more effective against the lower-flying B-24s at 21,000–23,000ft. General Otto von Renz, the RLM's Chief of Flak Development (*Flaktechnische Amt*), calculated that, even with radar direction, it took over 4,000 rounds to shoot down one American bomber. During most of 1943, flak accounted for almost half of the bombers lost over Germany, but by early 1944, Window and Carpet had significantly reduced the effectiveness of the Reich's heavy investment in anti-aircraft artillery, with less than 10 percent of American bombers being lost to flak.

By that time, it was obvious to the Luftwaffe leadership that its reliance on flak batteries to defend Germany was misguided. On February 5, 1944, Weise's Luftwaffebehlshaber Mitte was redesignated *Luftflotte Reich* (Reich Air Fleet), finally incorporating both fighters and flak into one organization, commanded by Generaloberst Hans-Jürgen Stumpff, an experienced air campaigner who had most recently led Luftflotte 5 in Operation *Barbarossa*, the Nazi invasion of Soviet Russia. Signaling the end of the flak arm's dominance of Germany's strategic air defense, Weise was transferred to the RLM, where he took over the Flaktechnische Amt.

Commanders

The Luftwaffe commander-in-chief (CinC) – and therefore the man responsible for the air defense of Germany – was Hermann Wilhelm Göring, a ruthless, power-hungry Prussian

Nazi politician with the veneer of wartime military aviation experience. Instrumental in negotiating Hitler's rise to Kanzler (*Chancellor*) in 1933, two years later he was rewarded by being appointed *Reichsluftfahrtminister* (Reich Minister for Aviation) and *Oberbefehlshaber* (CinC) of the Luftwaffe. Having none of the requisite attributes of a good commander and no talent, skill, or experience in making executive military decisions, initially he only exerted his authority over personnel moves and aircraft production.

Göring had not flown an aircraft since 1922 and lazily left doctrine, technological development, and combat operations to the professionals, at least until the wartime employment of "his air force" put his prestige at risk. His relationship with Hitler plateaued when his foolish, intrusive decision-making caused the Luftwaffe to lose the Battle of Britain. In November 1942, when he promised Hitler that the Luftwaffe could save General Friedrich Paulus' 6. Armee, surrounded at Stalingrad, through a sustained airlift of 300 sorties and 600 tonnes per day – and failed – he began an inexorable fall from grace. The avalanche of destruction caused during the RAF's five-month-long (March–July 1943) Battle of the Ruhr campaign caused the Nazi Party's civil leadership, and eventually Hitler, to turn against him, driving him into a reclusive but self-indulgent and decadent existence at his lavish Carinhall hunting estate, almost completely detached from the Luftwaffe's operations in defense of the Reich.

Generalfeldmarschall Hans-Jürgen Stumpff, commander of Luftflotte Reich. (NARA)

Ongoing operations, planning, and organization were left to Göring's COS, who from February 1939 was Generaloberst Hans Jeschonnek. A strident Nazi and Hitler-idolizer and an ardent ground attack/army support advocate, Jeschonnek's "rob Peter to pay Paul" policy of draining training units to expand operational forces at the outset of every new campaign eventually bankrupted the Luftwaffe. Increasingly blamed for his service's mounting air defense failures, Jeschonnek committed suicide on August 18, 1943, after 596 RAF heavy bombers pummeled the Peenemünde Army Research Centre on Germany's Baltic coast, attempting to disrupt Nazi secret weapon development. Replacing him was Generaloberst Günther Korten, the lackluster former commander of Luftflotte 1 who attempted to reverse his predecessor's anti-fighter bias.

Commanding the new Luftflotte Reich was Generaloberst Hans-Jürgen Stumpff. Son of an army officer, Stumpff was born in Kolberg (now Kołobrzeg, Poland) in 1889 and followed in his father's footsteps, joining the 2nd Brandenburg Grenadier Regiment, Prince Charles of Prussia, Nr. 12 at the age of 18. His natural military attributes were recognized early and, after being wounded on the front lines, he spent most of World War I on the General Staff, and afterwards was included in the 1,500 officers permitted by the Versailles Treaty to become members of the Weimar Republic's Reichswehr. Not particularly interested in military aviation – Stumpff was a personnel specialist – his organizational talents were nevertheless needed in the nascent, and soon burgeoning, Luftwaffe, into which he was transferred as an *oberstleutnant* (lieutenant colonel) in 1933. His skills at personnel management resulted in his appointment in June 1937 to be COS for Göring's ObdL (*Oberbefehlshaber der Luftwaffe*), ostensibly the Luftwaffe general staff and precursor to the OKL (*Oberkommando der Luftwaffe*).

Generalmajor Josef
"Beppo" Schmid,
commander of
I. Jagdkorps.
(Author's Collection)

Unable to tolerate or accommodate the ambitious and arrogant *Staatssekretär der Luftfahrt* (State Secretary for Aviation, Göring's deputy for running the RLM) Erhard Milch's intrusive involvement in Luftwaffe affairs, 18 months later Stumpff sought reassignment (being replaced by Jeschonnek) and was appointed *Inspekteur der Flakartillerie* (Inspector of Flak artillery). This ostensibly made him the Luftwaffe's Chief of Air Defenses, after which he commanded Luftflotte 1, based in Berlin, beginning in January 1940. That May – after the civilian technocrat Milch got his military command ticket punched by getting Göring to let him command Luftflotte 5 for 28 days – Stumpff took over and successfully concluded the Norwegian campaign that June. He commanded this northernmost Luftwaffe echelon against the Soviets – both in the far north and through Finland – during Operation *Barbarossa* (June 22 – December 5, 1941) and throughout the next two years. Untainted by the Luftwaffe's mounting failures, he was really the only viable officer qualified to command the defense of the Reich.

Commanding Stumpff's only operational force, I. Jagdkorps, was another non-pilot, former ObdL Chief of Intelligence, Generalmajor Josef "Beppo" (Boy) Schmid. A convivial Göring sycophant, Schmid was born in Göggingen, near Augsburg, in 1901. Too young to serve in World War I, Schmid joined Freikorps Epp (a right-wing paramilitary organization in Munich) in 1919, and two years later entered the Reichswehr as an officer cadet, joining the 19. Bayerische Infanterie-Regiment (19th Bavarian Infantry Regiment). An ardent young Nazi, he was one of the 2,000 who accompanied Hitler in the famous – and failed – Beer Hall Putsch.

Attending the infantry school at Munich at the end of 1924, he was assigned to the 21. Bayerische Infanterie-Regiment at Nuremburg, and after nine years' experience in various arms (mortar, machine gun, infantry), he attended General Staff training at the *Berlin Kriegsakademie* (War Academy). When Hitler ordered the wholesale expansion of the newly created Wehrmacht and formal establishment of the Luftwaffe in 1935, Schmid was transferred to the latter's Operations Department, where he worked – and was promoted – for four years. On April 1, 1939, he was selected as ObdL Chief of Intelligence but proved completely inept at the job, eventually paving the way for his chief to blunder into defeat in the Battle of Britain.

Nevertheless, in October 1942, he was rewarded for his excellent service by being named commander of the Luftwaffe's 1. Panzer-Division Hermann Göring. Formerly a brigade attached to the 11. Panzer-Division in the Ukraine, this unit was shipped to Tunisia and expanded to become a part of Generalfeldmarschall Ewin Rommel's Panzerarmee Afrika. Following the Allies' Operation *Torch* landings in North Africa and Montgomery's victory at the second battle of El Alamein, one defeat followed another, but Schmid was one of the few "special persons" evacuated immediately prior to the surrender of 244,500 troops (157,000 German, the remainder Italian) in Tunisia in May 1943. Promoted to major general and awarded the *Ritterkreuz des Eisernen Kreuzes* (Knight's Cross of the Iron Cross), he returned to work as Göring's advisor in the RLM before being rewarded again, this time with his assignment to command I. Jagdkorps.

CAMPAIGN OBJECTIVES

It had been a most gallant effort, but many, too many, had paid with their lives in disproving the Air Corps pre-war theory that the Flying Fortress could defend itself, unaided, against enemy fighters.

Colonel Richard D'Oyly Hughes, Eighth AF Assistant COS for Operations Plans, as stated in his *Memoirs*, 1956

The Eighth AF's participation in the Allied CBO finally got off to a good start in the summer of 1943, with American B-17s and B-24s striking U-boat construction yards at Bremen, Hamburg, and Kiel, destroying the Norsk Hydro aluminum production facility in Norway, wrecking the I. G. Farben synthetic rubber factory at Hüls, and damaging the Heinkel, Focke-Wulf, and Fieseler (producing Me 109s) factories at Warnemünde, Bremen, and Kassel.

Disturbingly, however, American losses were unexpectedly high. While a loss rate of 3.5 percent in 1942 was bad enough, during the first six months of the next year the average was 6.6 percent per mission. Ten percent per mission was considered the highest that could be sustained and have replacements and reinforcements fill the resulting gaps and still continue to build towards the goal of being able to launch 300 bombers per mission, the number Eighth AF chief Eaker believed, through massed defensive firepower, would prevent "excessive or uneconomical loss."

In August, Eighth AF planners attempted to increase the pace by launching four maximum effort, deep penetration missions. Libya-based Ninth AF B-24s, augmented by Eighth AF Liberators, would attack the Romanian oil refineries at Ploiești, followed by attacks against Schweinfurt ball-bearing plants and the Regensburg and Wiener Neustadt Messerschmitt factories, where 48 percent of Germany's single-engine fighters were made.

In the Ploiești strike (Operation *Tidal Wave*), two of the nine refineries were destroyed and two more damaged, temporarily cutting production by 40 percent. The follow-up

The concept that made the difference. Filmed during the October 2 raid on Emden, the USAAF documentary *Thunderbolt: Ramrod to Emden* featured 56th FG Thunderbolts escorting the 95th BG Fortresses, dramatically illustrating the escort fighter's potential. (NMUSAF *The Thunderbolts: Ramrod to Emden*)

OPPOSITE EIGHTH AIR FORCE RAID ON OSCHERSLEBEN 11TH JANUARY 1944

Called "the last victory of the Luftwaffe over the American Air Forces" by Schmid in his post-war history *The Struggle for Air Supremacy over the Reich*, the Eighth AF's strike on January 11, 1944, was a trial run for Operation *Argument*'s planned attacks on German aviation industry targets. It was the first deep penetration mission attempting to use the newly developed escort relay procedures all the way to the targets, in this case aircraft factories at Oschersleben, Halberstadt, and Braunschweig.

To aid in the bomber stream's penetration of Reich airspace, four P-47 fighter groups (FGs) were launched, one pair to escort the bombers across Holland and the second to cover their flanks from Arnhem to the Weser River. Because greater bomber losses typically occurred during egress, twice as many P-47 FGs were dispatched to provide withdrawal support in relays as depicted. The two P-38 groups were detailed to rendezvous with the 2nd and 3rd BDs over Braunschweig and escort them out of the target area. The single available P-51 unit (354th FG) was assigned to protect the 1st BD, its 49 P-51s splitting to escort the B-17s to both targets.

While adverse weather handicapped most of the operation – the 2nd BD was recalled at the Dutch border and most of the 3rd BD aborted from over Germany – the 1st BD's accurate visual bombing (51 percent hits) caused extensive devastation to Oschersleben's Fw 190A plant and less damage to the Ju 88 component factory at Halberstadt. However, the 354th FG's Mustangs rendezvoused ahead of schedule and were unable to stay with the bombers past the target, leaving the 1st BD unprotected from the targets to Bielefeld, resulting in 42 B-17s being lost (a 14.4 percent loss rate) in what was described as the "heaviest air fighting in the war."

Believing the raid was bound for Berlin, the Luftwaffe launched a maximum effort – 579 day- and night-fighters, of which 482 engaged the 313 B-17s that made it to their targets. Of these, 58 (12 percent) were lost, of which 31 were claimed by escorting fighters. Only one P-38 and four P-47s were lost in combat, establishing a 6:1 dominance over the defending interceptors. However, the large gaps in escort coverage resulted in serious bomber losses, so VIII Fighter Command planners made several changes to ensure that the fighter coverage was more continuous for the bomber formations, especially entering and egressing from the target area, where Luftwaffe attacks were fiercest and losses were the greatest.

strike against the Wiener Neustadter Flugzeugwerke AG fighter factory (Operation *Juggler*) temporarily cut their Me 109 production from 270 to 184 for one month.

The Eighth AF's dual Schweinfurt–Regensburg mission was moderately successful. At Schweinfurt, 80 direct hits (of 954 bombs dropped) destroyed 36 percent of two factories' manufacturing capabilities, cutting production by more than half (from 140 tons monthly to 119 in August and September combined) for the next six weeks. The Regensburg attack destroyed or seriously damaged six of the eight Messerschmitt workshops, temporarily reducing production by 35 percent.

However, during the course of these four missions, a total of 119 bombers were lost, with 1,079 men killed, captured, or missing – a 20.6 percent loss rate. The participating bomb groups were so decimated that it took two months to recover their strength.

"Black Week" – the crisis of American daylight strategic bombing

By October, VIII BC had recovered sufficiently to launch a tightly spaced series of deep penetration missions, culminating in a second – and equally disastrous – Schweinfurt attack. These raids virtually destroyed the Arado aircraft component plant at Anklam and heavily damaged the Focke-Wulf factory at Marienburg. Also hit – but with less effect – were shipyards at Bremen and Danzig/Gdynia (Gdańsk), and road and railroad complexes at/ near Münster. At Schweinfurt, 12.7 percent of bombs hit within the ball-bearing factory complexes (with 88 being direct hits), destroying another 31 percent of production capacity.

Called "Black Week," American losses – out of 1,211 effective sorties – were 173 bombers lost with 1,499 men killed, wounded, or missing, an overall attrition rate of 14.3 percent. It was a Pyrrhic victory of epic proportions. Disturbed by continued unsustainable losses, Arnold recognized that drastic solutions were needed, and the Eighth AF would not be back until the fixes were in the works. A complete overhaul of the Eighth AF, its leadership, its mission objectives, and VIII FC's (VIII Fighter Command) doctrine and equipment were necessary to pull out of the disastrous tail spin that threatened to prematurely terminate the American experiment in daylight precision bombing.

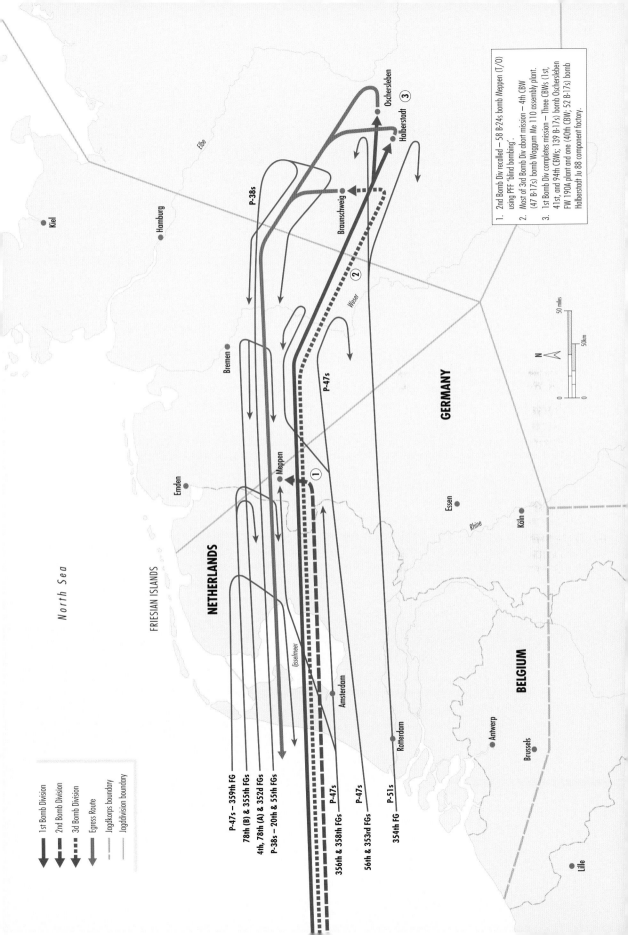

North Sea

FRIESIAN ISLANDS

Kiel

Hamburg

Elbe

Emden

Bremen

NETHERLANDS

Ijsselmeer

Amsterdam

Meppen ①

P-38s

Braunschweig

Weser

②

Oschersleben ③

Holberstadt

P-47s

GERMANY

Essen

Rhine

Köln

Rotterdam

Antwerp

Brussels

BELGIUM

Lille

1. 2nd Bomb Div recalled – 58 B-24s bomb Meppen (T/O) using PFF 'blind bombing'.

2. Most of 3rd Bomb Div abort mission – 4th CBW (47 B-17s) bomb Waggum Me 110 assembly plant.

3. 1st Bomb Div completes mission – Three CBWs (1st, 41st, and 94th CBWs; 139 B-17s) bomb Oschersleben FW 190A plant and one (40th CBW; 52 B-17s) bomb Halberstadt Ju 88 component factory.

N

50 miles

50km

0

1st Bomb Division
2nd Bomb Division
3d Bomb Division
Egress Route
Jagdkorps boundary
Jagddivision boundary

P-47s – 359th FG
78th (B) & 355th FGs
4th, 78th (A) & 352d FGs
P-38s – 20th & 55th FGs
356th & 358th FGs — P-47s
56th & 353rd FGs — P-47s
354th FG — P-51s

The Eighth AF's devastating attack on the Focke-Wulf factory at Marienburg on October 9, 1943, was cited as one of the most effective bombing missions to date – and demonstrated what high altitude daylight precision bombing could do in near perfect circumstances: 48 percent of 598 bombs impacted within the factory complex, with 35 direct hits on buildings and facilities. (NMUSAF 050603-F-1234P-001)

Apparent to everyone but Eaker and his VIII FC commander, Brigadier General Frank O'Driscoll Hunter, was that escort fighters – shepherding the misnamed Fortresses all the way to their targets and back – were the solution to the crisis. Consequently, Arnold had to step in and solve the problem. First to go was Hunter, who valued exciting but unproductive fighter sweeps over the "wasteful" (his word) and tedious task of escorting bombers. Eaker tried to save Hunter, but that only convinced Arnold that he "didn't get it either."

But Hap knew the key was fighters escorting the bombers all the way to the targets and back, so he ordered all P-38 and P-51 units deploying to combat theaters to be reassigned to Kepner's VIII FC for the next three months. This allowed new Mustang units to be transferred to England to convert five VIII FC Thunderbolt groups (4th, 352nd, 355th, 359th, and 361st) to P-51B/Cs. As an expedient, two new P-38 groups were sent to the Eighth AF instead of the Mediterranean and Pacific.

Finally, with a second strategic air force established in Italy and long-range escort fighter units flying into England, the last thing needed was to appoint a leader who would get the job done. Convinced that Eaker did not understand or appreciate the need for – and urgency of – attaining air superiority over Western Europe by defeating the Luftwaffe, on January 6, Arnold reassigned the Eighth AF commander to the Mediterranean, replacing him with Doolittle.

One of the new commander's first edicts was to correct the mission statement of VIII FC from "the primary role of all US Fighter units [is the] support and protection of Heavy Bombers engaged in Pointblank" to "the first duty of Eighth Air Force fighters is to destroy German fighters." To Kepner, he added, "We'll still provide a reasonable fighter escort for the bombers, but the bulk of your fighters will go hunting for Jerries [Germans]. Flush them out in the air and beat them up on the ground on the way home. Your first priority is to take the offensive."

The Luftwaffe's response

Meanwhile, unbeknownst to American leadership, I. Jagdkorps was having a crisis of its own. During "Black Week," the approximately 2,050 effective interceptor sorties (those that engaged the enemy) cost 80 fighters, 44 of which were claimed by P-47s (for five losses) that were now escorting the bombers all the way across Belgium and Holland.

Additionally, the extended series of damaging attacks against airfields in northern France, Belgium, and western Holland by Eighth/Ninth AF Martin B-26 Marauders – as well as occasional raids by heavy bombers – conducted as part of Operation *Starkey*, the deception campaign designed to convince the Nazis that the cross-Channel invasion would land in the Boulogne area, between August and October 1943, made Luftwaffe operations from forward area airfields almost untenable. Schmid reacted by withdrawing his single-engine fighter units back into eastern Holland and the Rhine area, and ordered Generalmajor Walter Grabmann's 3. Jagddivision to delay battle until the P-47 escorts had turned for home.

In December, Schmid reorganized the Reich's air defense system, reassigning flak units from their original Luftgau to the Jagddivision for better coordination between fighter and flak forces. Operationally, to meet the steadily rising size of American bomber formations – as well as their increasing number of escorts – he directed the Jagddivisionen to start using *Gefechtsverbände* (battle formations) of two or three Gruppen, approximately 60–90 fighters, and to concentrate their intercepts on one point on the bomber stream in order to gain numerical superiority at the point of attack.

Additionally, signaling the shift in the Luftwaffe's weight of effort countering the Allies' round the clock bombing campaign from battling RAF Bomber Command to meeting the Eighth AF's more destructive daylight bombing, Schmid ordered Oberst Hans-Joachim "Hajo" Herrmann's 30. Jagddivision of single-engine night-fighters – nicknamed Wild Sau – to reinforce the RLV's day-fighter resources. Relying on searchlights to illuminate the RAF night-bombers at night, Herrmann's Wild Sau units were only marginally successful. However, they were manned by former bomber, transport, and instructor pilots who had training and experience flying on instruments at night and in bad weather. With the onset of increasingly adverse winter weather, these flight skills were badly needed in the daytime battles.

Day-fighter pilots had only the most rudimentary blind flying instruments in their cockpits and lacked any appreciable instrument training. Losses of day-fighters in weather-related accidents accounted for as much as half of the total during periods of reduced visibility, low

Major General Frederick L. Anderson was the architect of Operation *Argument*. He had previously commanded the 4th Bombardment Wing at Marks Hall from May 1943, after which he was appointed commander of VIII BC on July 1, 1943, before being named as General Spaatz's deputy for operations in January 1944. (NMUSAF)

OPPOSITE POTENTIAL AVIATION INDUSTRY TARGETS IN NAZI GERMANY, JANUARY 1944

ceilings, thick clouds, and icing conditions. The ongoing battle was so desperate that there was no time to send these experienced interceptor pilots to instrument training schools, so Hermann's Wild Sau units were tasked to teach these badly needed skills to several operational Jagdwaffe units. For example, on February 18, 1944 – only two days before Operation *Argument* was launched – III./JG 3 was transferred from Bad Wörishofen to Leipheim to undergo instrument training administered by the pilots of I./JG 301.

Operation *Argument* planning

The 354th FG's Lieutenant Colonel James Howard in the cockpit of his North American Aviation P-51B-5-NA Mustang, S/N 43-6315, DING HAO! at RAF Boxted, April 25, 1944. Howard was awarded the Medal of Honor for single-handedly protecting a formation of 401st BG B-17s from ravaging attacks by Me 110G Zerstörers, shooting down four, during the Eighth AF's January 11, 1944, raid on Oschersleben. (USAF HRA)

In preparation for the Churchill–Roosevelt Cairo Conference (codename Sextant, November 22–26), the CCS's Combined Operations Planning Committee conducted a thorough review and assessment of *Pointblank*. Operationally, the CBO had proven faithful to its defining guidance: Eighth and Ninth AFs had hit Luftwaffe aircraft factories, ball-bearing plants, oil refineries, U-boat shipyards, and transportation complexes. But prioritizing the German aircraft industry as simply "second to none" was having little noticeable – and no advantageous – effect.

From the Sextant Conference, the CCS confirmed that "the present plan for the Combined Bomber Offensive should remain unchanged" but ordered a "revision of the bombing objectives." Three days later, Eighth AF and RAF Bomber Command were directed to plan an intensive, week-long, maximum effort bombing campaign against German fighter production facilities, which during the second half of 1943 had produced an average of 851 aircraft each month. For 1944, RLM deputy and *Generalluftzeugmeister*

● Aviation-related industries
▲ Airframe component and final assembly factories
⁘ Anti-friction ball and roller-bearing producers

Kiel

Rostock
▲ Marienehe Heinkel Flugzeugwerke
HQ, He 111s and He 219s

Tutow
▲ Focke-Wulf Flugzeugbau AG
FW 190As

Hamburg

Elbe

Bremen
▲ Focke-Wulf Flugzeugbau AG
HQ and FW 190As

Oschersleben
▲ AGO Flugzeugwerke AG
FW 190A assembly
▲ Junkers Zweigwerk Oschersleben
Ju 188 fuselages

Oranienburg
▲ Heinkel-Werke GmbH Oranienburg
He 111s and He 177s

Berlin
⁘ VKF's Erkner Factory
Anti-friction bearings
⁘ Norddeutsche Kugellager Fabrik
Anti-friction bearings

Braunschweig
● Muhlenbau-Industrie AG
DB 605B engines

Brandenburg
● Arado Flugzeugwerke GmbH
He 177 components

Weser

Münster

Halberstadt
▲ Junkers Zweigwerk Halberstadt
Ju 88/188 wings and tails

Dessau
▲ Junkers-Flugzeugwerk AG
HQ and Ju 188s

Aschersleben
▲ Junkers Zweigwerk Aschersleben
Ju 88 fuselages

Essen

Kassel
▲ Gerhard Fieseler Werke GmbH
Me 109Gs

Bernburg
▲ Junkers Flugzeug-und-
Motorwerk GmbH
Ju 88C/G and Ju 188 assembly

Leipzig
▲ ATG and Erla-Maschinenwerke GmbH
Me 109G assembly
● Junkers Motorenwerke GmbH
Jumo 213 engines

Köln

Gotha
▲ Gothaer Waggonfabrik AG
Me 110Gs and Me 410s

Rhine

Koblenz

Mosel

GERMANY

Schweinfurt
⁘ Vereinigte Kugellager Fabriken (VKF)
Anti-friction bearings

Main

Fürth
▲ Bachmann-von Blumenthal Flugzeugbau
Me 110Gs

Nürnberg

FRANCE

Regensburg
▲ Messerschmitt AG
Me 109Gs

Stuttgart
● Daimler AG
HQ and DB 605 engines
⁘ AB Svenska Kullagerfabriken
Anti-friction bearings

Rhine

Oberpfaffenhofen
▲ Dornier Flugzeugwerke
Do 217s

Danube

Augsburg
▲ Messerschmitt AG
HQ and Me 109Gs

Munich

N

0   50 miles

0   50km

(General in charge of aircraft production) Erhard Milch had increased the monthly production goal to 2,000 single-engine and 250 twin-engine interceptors. For the Luftwaffe to be crippled prior to Operation *Overlord*, these rates had to be reduced as much as possible.

Coordinating closely with the USAAF Economic Warfare Division's Enemy Objectives Unit (EOU), the VIII BC staff – led by their commander, Major General Frederick L. Anderson (soon moved to USSTAF as Spaatz's deputy for operations) – planned to strike aircraft component/sub-assembly factories and aero-engine manufacturers, as well as aircraft final assembly plants. The first day's missions – attacking targets at or near Braunschweig, Leipzig, and Tutow – were aimed against factories that produced 70 percent of the Luftwaffe's single-engine fighters, 90 percent of its twin-engine Zerstörers and night-fighters, and 60 percent of its bombers.

In conjunction, the now-UK-based Ninth AF would coordinate its short-range bombing missions against Luftwaffe airfields and V-1 "buzz bomb" launch sites in Belgium, Holland, and northern France as diversions designed to draw off the forward-deployed JG 2 and JG 26. To make the effort truly combined, the RAF would be killing factory workers – and other civilians – in the same areas during the week-long campaign.

Preparing for this sustained aerial offensive, Doolittle carefully husbanded his bomber forces, turning down nonessential missions "to avoid having the hammerhead force depleted between critical operations." By January, the Eighth AF had amassed 1,304 operational heavy bombers and 1,405 crews, with an additional 2,322 aircraft in the supply channels. This permitted the bomber groups' establishment to be increased from 36 to 48 aircraft, allowing each bombardment division to assemble combat wings of 54 (B-24s) to 60 (B-17s) bombers for maximum effectiveness. Anticipating losing 200 bombers on each day's deep penetration missions, the stockpile of over 2,000 aeroplanes was reassuring – it was the aircrews that were the limiting factor.

Ever the thinking man's aviator commander, unlike the USAAF's dyed in the wool bomber advocates, Doolittle knew that bombing Luftwaffe's fighter factories was not as important as destroying Jagdwaffe interceptors in the air. As he said later, "German fighter production, which had long been one of our first priority targets, no longer really mattered … since the [Jagdwaffe] could no longer use the products for lack of fuel and trained replacement pilots."

By January, his VIII FC had a dozen fighter groups (including one of P-51s and two with P-38s) with 1,254 operational fighters and 1,140 pilots, with 2,571 more fighters in the supply pipeline. This permitted Kepner to increase his fighter groups' establishment from 75 to 108 aircraft, allowing each unit to launch two 36-aeroplane formations (three four-plane flights for each squadron) – known as A and B Groups – instead of the previous single 48-fighter formations.

Against these, at the beginning of February, Schmid's I. Jagdkorps had on hand 530 single-engine interceptors, 80 twin-engine Zerstörers, and 545 night-fighters, some of which could be used against the American daylight missions. By mid-February, attrition and serviceability issues, according to Schmid, had reduced his effective forces to 350 operational single-engine interceptors and, due to sustained RAF night-bombing operations, only 50 twin-engine night-fighters were available to augment his 80 Zerstörers.

The plan was in place and the American forces were ready by January 1, but the planned week-long offensive required a stable clear-air, high-pressure weather system to dominate continental Europe. Initiating the offensive was scheduled repeatedly, but each time deteriorating winter weather forced its cancellation. At long last, on Friday, February 18, 1944, came the break that Spaatz, Doolittle, and Anderson were looking for. Two extensive high pressure areas were detected – one developing over the Baltic, the other just west of Ireland – that between them would break up the nearly incessant cloud cover and create at least three days of clear skies beginning on Sunday, February 20.

THE CAMPAIGN

If bombers are not being attacked groups will detach one or two squadrons to range out searching for enemy aircraft. Upon withdrawal, if endurance permits, groups will search for and destroy enemy aircraft in the air and on the ground.

Major General William E. Kepner, VIII Fighter Command Field Order,
February 8, 1944

Eighth AF Mission 226, February 20

Dawn on February 20 found the 930-year old medieval trading city of Leipzig – in 1944 the sixth largest metropolis in the Greater German Reich – blanketed with a pristine mantle of new-fallen snow. But its beauty was badly marred by hundreds of ugly craters and the blackened smoking ruins caused by RAF Bomber Command's rain of destruction only hours before.

Operation *Argument* actually began in the small hours (0315 to 0420hrs) of the morning when some 730 RAF heavy bombers – having lost ten in mid-air collisions en route to the target – dumped over 2,500 tons of bombs and incendiaries on the city, killing 930 inhabitants. None of the city's outlying aircraft factories were targeted – the purpose of the RAF night attack, in addition to killing civilians and destroying their homes, was to fatigue the local flak crews and exhaust their ammunition in anticipation of the Eighth AF's first mission of what was to become known in military aviation history as "Big Week." This cannon fodder mission cost the RAF an additional 69 bombers shot down by Luftwaffe night-fighters and flak, with a total of 551 crewmen lost (420 killed and 131 captured), while paving the way for the Americans' first big strike.

The focus of the offensive's first day were large aircraft airframe and aero-engine industries near Leipzig, Braunschweig, and Posen, each to be attacked by one of Doolittle's three heavy

A 56th FG P-47 taking off from RAF Halesworth in 1943. The Thunderbolt was the heaviest and most powerful of all fighters engaged in the European Theatre of Operations in 1944 and quickly dominated its Luftwaffe opponents, at least as far as its limited range would permit. (NMUSAF)

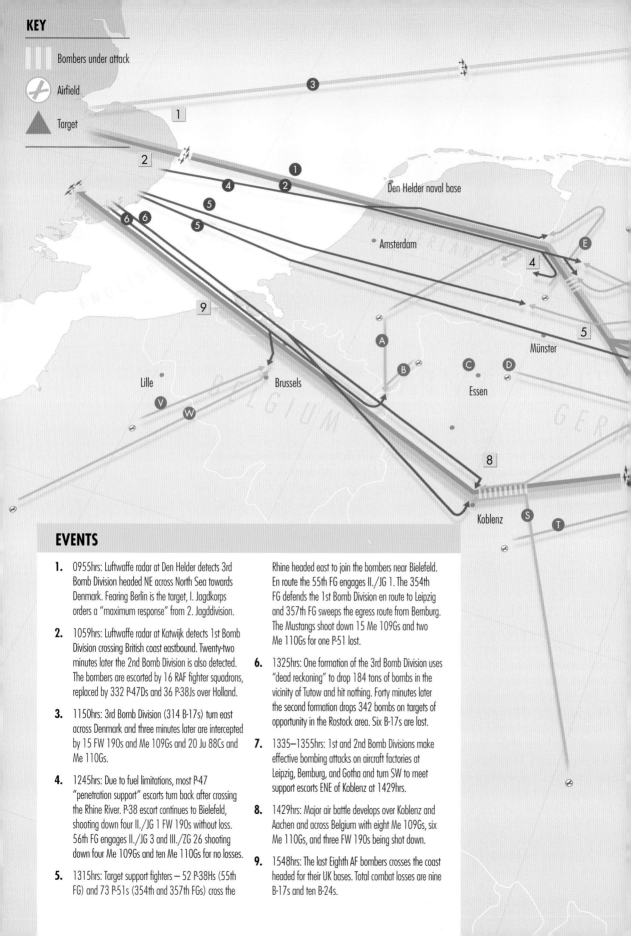

KEY

||| Bombers under attack

◈ Airfield

▲ Target

Den Helder naval base

Amsterdam

Münster

Lille

Brussels

Essen

Koblenz

EVENTS

1. 0955hrs: Luftwaffe radar at Den Helder detects 3rd Bomb Division headed NE across North Sea towards Denmark. Fearing Berlin is the target, I. Jagdkorps orders a "maximum response" from 2. Jagddivision.

2. 1059hrs: Luftwaffe radar at Katwijk detects 1st Bomb Division crossing British coast eastbound. Twenty-two minutes later the 2nd Bomb Division is also detected. The bombers are escorted by 16 RAF fighter squadrons, replaced by 332 P-47Ds and 36 P-38Js over Holland.

3. 1150hrs: 3rd Bomb Division (314 B-17s) turn east across Denmark and three minutes later are intercepted by 15 FW 190s and Me 109Gs and 20 Ju 88Cs and Me 110Gs.

4. 1245hrs: Due to fuel limitations, most P-47 "penetration support" escorts turn back after crossing the Rhine River. P-38 escort continues to Bielefeld, shooting down four II./JG 1 FW 190s without loss. 56th FG engages II./JG 3 and III./ZG 26 shooting down four Me 109Gs and ten Me 110Gs for no losses.

5. 1315hrs: Target support fighters — 52 P-38Hs (55th FG) and 73 P-51s (354th and 357th FGs) cross the

Rhine headed east to join the bombers near Bielefeld. En route the 55th FG engages II./JG 1. The 354th FG defends the 1st Bomb Division en route to Leipzig and 357th FG sweeps the egress route from Bernburg. The Mustangs shoot down 15 Me 109Gs and two Me 110Gs for one P-51 lost.

6. 1325hrs: One formation of the 3rd Bomb Division uses "dead reckoning" to drop 184 tons of bombs in the vicinity of Tutow and hit nothing. Forty minutes later the second formation drops 342 bombs on targets of opportunity in the Rostock area. Six B-17s are lost.

7. 1335–1355hrs: 1st and 2nd Bomb Divisions make effective bombing attacks on aircraft factories at Leipzig, Bernburg, and Gotha and turn SW to meet support escorts ENE of Koblenz at 1429hrs.

8. 1429hrs: Major air battle develops over Koblenz and Aachen and across Belgium with eight Me 109Gs, six Me 110Gs, and three FW 190s being shot down.

9. 1548hrs: The last Eighth AF bombers crosses the coast headed for their UK bases. Total combat losses are nine B-17s and ten B-24s.

First Day of 'Big Week': Operation *Argument*, 20 February 1944

Operation *Argument* began with an extensive, complicated mission involving 985 bombers and 835 escort fighters. Each of the Eighth AF's three bomb division was assigned two or three major aircraft industry targets, two of them in eastern Germany. The main attack – against five targets in north central Germany – was provided with nearly continuous and highly effective penetration, target area, and withdrawal fighter support, resulting in significant Luftwaffe losses.

Kiel

Hamburg

Rostock

Stralsund

6

Greifswald

Tutow

Braunschweig

Stetten

Halberstadt

Oschersleben

Berlin

Bernburg

Luchenwalde

7

Gotha

Leipzig

POLAND

Poznań

Major Eighth AF Units: ●

1. 1st Bombardment Division (B-17s)
2. 2nd Bombardment Division (B-24s)
3. 3rd Bombardment Division (B-17s)
4. Penetration Support – 20th FG (P-38s), 56th FG, 353rd FG, 356th FG, 358th FG, 359th FG, 360th FG, and 361st FG (P-47s)
5. Target Area Support – 55th FG (P-38s), 354th and 357th FGs (P-51s)
6. Withdrawal – 55th FG (P-38s), 4th FG, 78th FG, 352nd FG, 355th FG, 356th FG, 361st FG, and 362nd FG (P-47s)

Luftwaffe Interceptor Units: ●

3. Jagddivision

A.	III./JG 1	Volkel
B.	IV./JG 3	Venlo
C.	I./JG 3	Mönchen-Gladbach (deployed to Volkel)
D.	I./JG 1	Dortmund
E.	II./JG 1	Rheine

2. Jagddivision

F.	I./JG 11	Husum
G.	II./JG 11 and III./ZG 26	Wunstorf
H.	III./JG 11	Oldenburg
I.	II./JG 3	Rotenburg a/d Wümme
J.	II./NJG 3	Schleswig
K.	III./NJG 3	Stade
L.	II./ZG 26	Hildesheim
M.	I./ZG 26	Völkenrode

1. Jagddivision

N.	III./JG 54	Ludwigslust
O.	II./NJG 5	Parchim
P.	II./NJG 6	Stendal
Q.	I./JG 302	Jüterbog
R.	I. and II./ZG 76 with I./NJG 6	Delitsch

7. Jagddivision

S.	III./JG 3	Leipheim
T.	II./JG 27	Wiesbaden
U.	I./JG 301	Neubiburg

4. Jagddivision

V.	II./JG 26	Cambrai-Epinoy

5. Jagddivision

W.	III./JG 2	Cormeilles-en-Vixen

bomber divisions – over 1,000 B-17s and B-24s. Anderson's plan of attack was to have the Eighth's main force – about 420 Flying Fortresses from the 1st Bombardment Division and 280 2nd Bombardment Division Liberators – fly deep into Germany to bomb aircraft industry targets around Leipzig and Braunschweig, respectively, while the 3rd Bombardment Division's long-ranged B-17s struck targets in eastern Germany.

Approaching from the south, Twining's Fifteenth AF was to strike the large Messerschmitt Me 109G assembly plant at Regensburg-Obertraubling, but could only provide 126 B-17s from the 5th Bombardment Wing (BW) because the other two BWs, both flying B-24 Liberators, were needed to support a renewed Allied ground offensive hoping to break out from the Anzio beachhead just south of Rome. As it turned out, over the Alps the bombers encountered icing conditions so severe that they were forced to turn back and abandon the mission.

Flying more than 525 miles to Leipzig, Major General Robert William's 1st Bomb Division sent four combat wings – almost 360 Flying Fortresses, designated the 1st Task Force – to bomb four *Allgemeine Transportanlagen Gesellschaft* (ATG, or General Transportation Equipment Company) factories. Three of them, in the suburbs of Abtnaundorf, Aschersleben, and Heiterblick, made Me 109G components for Erla-Maschinenwerke GmbH, which were assembled at Leipzig's large Mockau airfield. Erla provided 32 per cent of the Luftwaffe's monthly Me 109G production. A fifth combat wing of about 60 B-17s would hit the Junkers Flugzeug-und-Motorenwerke AG's Ju 88/Ju 188 assembly plant at Bernburg.

Flying a parallel route offset about 10 miles to the south, and initially 20 minutes behind the leading B-17s, was the 2nd Task Force, Major General James P. Hodges' Norfolk-based B-24 Liberators. They would accompany the Flying Fortresses 440 miles, to overhead Bielefeld, where the five combat wings would fan out to strike four targets. Two were to attack the two Muhlenbau-Industrie AG (MIAG) plants at Braunschweig manufacturing DB 605B engines and airframe component parts for the Me 110G, while the third would bomb the Junkers Zweigwerk Halberstadt, making Ju 88 wings and tail sections. The two other combat wings would fly 60 miles further to the southeast to attack the Gothaer Waggonfabrik (GWF) final assembly plant, then the Luftwaffe's largest Me 110G and Me 410 producer.

The 700 bombers would be provided with heavy VIII Fighter Command penetration support – 332 P-47s and 36 P-38s – to get them through the outer crust of the RLV's fighter defenses, Grabmann's 3. Jagddivision. Target support over Braunschweig and Leipzig would be 52 P-38s (55th FG) and 73 Mustangs (354th and 357th FGs), respectively. Withdrawal support for both forces would consist of another 336 Thunderbolts and 30 Lightnings.

Because the massive force initially headed directly towards Berlin, hopes were high that it would attract the bulk of I. Jagdkorps' fighter response. This would permit Major General Curtis E. LeMay's Suffok-based 3rd Bomb Division – 314 unescorted B-17s – to be sent across the North Sea and Denmark to strike targets east of Berlin with minimum interference. These were the huge Luftwaffe engineering facility at Tutow, bomber crew training center at Kreising airfield, and the Fw 190 factory complex at Krzesiny, a suburb of Poznań. Called Posen under Nazi occupation, this historically Polish city was located 140 miles inland from the Baltic Sea coast. To avoid civilian casualties, the lead bombardiers were instructed to abort their attacks if weather conditions did not

Having used radio beacons to assemble their combat wing high above an expansive overcast over England, the 1st Bombardment Division's 381st BG begin their long flight deep into Germany to attack the four Me 109G component and assembly plants at Leipzig. (NMUSAF)

permit visual bombing. In that case, Heinkel Flugzeugwerke facilities at Stettin (now Szczecin, Poland) and Rostock were secondary targets.

After assembling the six combat wings over East Anglia, LeMay's force flew in two large formations fairly close together and the massive radar return showed up on 3. Jagddivision coastal radars about 75 miles west of the Dutch naval base at Den Helder at 0955hrs. Estimated as "approximately 150 bombers," the coastal radar chain followed their progress northeast for two hours until they approached the Danish coast near Esbjerg. Fearing that the Americans were attempting an end around maneuver to attack Berlin from over the North Sea, from 1035–1048hrs Generalmajor Max-Josef Ibel launched Oberstleutant Hermann Graf's JG 11 – some 70 Me 109Gs and Fw 190As – with orders to rendezvous over Fredenbeck, just southwest of Stade. These were to be reinforced by 25 new Me 410s (II./ZG 26) – led by 34-victory ace Hauptmann Eduard Tratt, the Luftwaffe's highest-scoring Zerstörer Experte – and 19 Fw 190As (II./JG 1), all launching with instructions to join Graf's Gefechtsverband.

At the Danish coast, LeMay's Fortresses turned almost due east to head across the Jutland peninsula, Fünen, and Zealand. Not waiting for his reinforcements, at 11534hrs Graf intercepted with his Stab (staff) flight and I./JG 11 – a mixed bag of about 15 Gustavs and Focke-Wulfs – followed by approximately 20 Ju 88Cs (II./NJG 3) and Me 110Gs (III./NJG 3) from Schleswig and Stade.

A running battle was fought across Denmark, but results were poor for the Germans. Graf's initial intercept force shot down two B-17Gs (388th BG), but lost two fighters to the Fortresses' defensive fire. Meanwhile Hauptmann Anton "Toni" Hackl's III./JG 11 and Hauptmann Hermann Seegatz's II./JG 1 were recalled to Oldenburg to engage what was soon determined to be the primary threat.

Intercepting over Fünen and Zealand at 1215–1225hrs, Tratt's Me 410s claimed to shoot down two B-17Gs, Tratt being credited with downing a 452nd BG Fortress (reportedly lost to a rocket-firing Ju 88C) over Korsør, Denmark, killing eight crewmen. Immediately afterwards, he disengaged to lead his Zerstörergruppe back to Hildesheim to refuel and rearm to meet the main threat, approaching from the west.

Due to the extensive undercast of clouds at 3,000ft blanketing Denmark, Schleswig-Holstein, and Germany's Baltic coast, half of LeMay's force navigated strictly by dead-reckoning (heading and time), and from somewhere overhead Zealand they turned southeast. The solid undercast continued to the south so at 1325hrs, unable to locate their targets, 105 Fortresses dropped their loads through the expansive cloud decks in the vicinities of Tutow, Greifswald, and Stralsund and did no appreciable damage.

Another 191 B-17s flew all the way to Poznań only to find it cloaked in cloud cover, so made a circling climb to the left to dump their loads – RAF-style – upon Rostock at 1400–1405hrs and other targets of opportunity (T/Os) on the way home. After flying 600 miles, enduring the biting and bitterly frigid cold for five hours, 506 tons of HE (high explosive) bombs and 202 tons of incendiaries were dropped "by guess and by golly" on nothing of any military significance.

Returning across Denmark, LeMay's Fortresses were intercepted by Major Rolf-Günther Hermichen's I./JG 11, reinforced with a few 10./JG 11 Fw 190As, shooting down one

Generalmajor Walter Grabmann, seen here as the commander of ZG 76 in June 1940, was a Zerstörer ace with an six confirmed victories, including five during the Battle of Britain. After 110 combat missions, in 1941 he was appointed commander of Zerstörerschule 2; the next year he was named JaFü Holland, and became commander of 3. Jagddivision in November 1943. (Author's Collection)

Stepping out of the cockpit of his P-47D Thunderbolt, Lieutenant Colonel Francis "Gabby" Gabreski (56th FG Operations Officer) is congratulated by Major Sylvester V. Burke. Burke led the 56th FG's Group A on the February 20 mission during which Gabreski shot down two Zerstörers, bringing his score to 13 victories. (NARA Ref 342-FH-3A12139-27448AC)

100th BG B-17G and damaging another, which crash-landed in Sweden. The 3rd Bomb Division's last stragglers cleared the Danish coastline north of Sylt at 1503hrs, beginning their three-hour journey across the North Sea to return to their bases. Altogether, six B-17s were lost, including one (390th BG) that crashed due to fuel exhaustion.

About an hour after LeMay's division was reported over the North Sea, at 1059hrs, the leading combat wing of Williams' 1st Task Force was detected 124 miles west of Egmond aan Zee, just crossing the East Anglian coastline eastbound, with an RAF escort of two Mustang and 14 Spitfire squadrons.

Trailing slightly, the 2nd Task Force's first combat wing also showed up on radar, causing the controllers at the 3. Jagddivision's Jägerleit Gefechtsstand control center at Deelen much alarm. They estimated the American force strength at "450 bombers, accompanied by a fighter escort" and it was pointed directly at Berlin. This was obviously the Eighth AF's major effort, so Grabmann scrambled I./JG 3 from Volkel, recalled Seegatz's II./JG 1 from northern Germany, and requested reinforcements from Ibel's 2. Jagddivision.

Taking off at noon, Hauptmann Josef Haiböck's I./JG 3 intercepted the 2nd Task Force's B-24s at the Dutch–German border but found themselves greatly outnumbered by the two groups of P-47s escorting them. Haiböck, a 60-victory ace from the Eastern Front, wisely decided not to engage and, approaching Meppen, he turned away, leading his heavily armed – but not so maneuverable – Me 109Gs back to Volkel.

Just past Meppen, the massive phalanx of bombers angled southeast towards Bielefeld and the last pair of Thunderbolt groups turned back for England at 1245hrs, replaced by the 20th (P-38Js) and 56th (P-47Ds) FGs. Colonel Bart Russell's 29 Lightnings were nearing their rendezvous with the bombers when they spotted a smaller formation of single-engine fighters approaching from the northeast. These were nine Fw 190s – a Staffel from Seegatz's II./JG 1 – that had taken off from Oldenburg at 1300hrs. Quickly overwhelmed, four were shot down, with two pilots killed. The 20th FG lost no P-38s in these combats.

Meanwhile, at 1135hrs, Ibel scrambled Hauptmann Detlev Rohwer's II./JG 3 from Rotenburg an der Wümme and, to provide the Pulk Zerstörers to break up the American bomber formations, these were followed 38 minutes later by two Staffeln of Major Johann "Hans" Kogler's III./ZG 26 from Wunstorf. The 13 Me 110G-2s were ordered to take off individually, climb out through the 1,500–4,800ft cloud deck, and form up at 12,000ft over Dümmer Lake, a prominent landmark visible through the breaks in the undercast.

Unfortunately for the Zerstörers, they were spotted by the veteran 56th FG, the Eighth's highest-scoring fighter unit with over 220 victories to its credit. Flying for the first time with the new locally fabricated 150-gallon drop tanks that extended the endurance of the "Jug" by another 15 minutes and pushed its combat radius to Hannover, the 56th FG flew in two combat groups, the first consisting of the 61st and 63rd Fighter Squadrons (FS). Major Sylvester Burke (63rd FS CO) led Group A to Dümmer Lake, joining on the 1st Bomb Division's northern flank at 22,000ft.

About 30 miles west of Hannover, a wingman of Lieutenant Colonel Francis "Gabby" Gabreski (11-victory ace and 56th FG Operations Officer) called "tally ho" on ZG 26's Me 110s, at seven o'clock about 7,000ft below. Gabreski wheeled his 61st FS formation around to the left and dived out of the sun, his 12 Thunderbolts roaring down in three flights, one after another. Gabreski shot down two of the Zerstörers in quick succession as the 61st FS began massacring Kogler's formation. Altogether, III./ZG 26 lost ten Me 110Gs destroyed and three damaged, with 11 aircrew killed and six wounded.

Following about 20 minutes behind Burke's A Group, Major David Schilling (former 62nd FS CO, now 56th FG Flying Executive) led 56th FG's B Group to join the 2nd Task Force near Minden. They arrived to find Hodges' Liberators being intercepted by Rohwer's II./JG 3 and broke up the attacks, shooting down four Gustavs, killing one pilot and wounding the other three. The 56th FG lost no P-47s in these combats.

Meanwhile, taking off from Wunstorf at noon were II./JG 11's Gustavs, who were ordered to form up above the clouds using a radio beacon near Münster. Having crossed the Dutch coast at 1309hrs, Major Mark Shipman was leading the 55th FG's 52 P-38Hs, intending to rendezvous with Hodges' Liberators at Bielefeld and provide target support around Braunschwieg. However, about 30 miles west of Münster, some 20 Me 109Gs were sighted above, while an additional 40 were seen climbing out of the undercast below. Shipman decided that "the dispersal of the 109s was of greater importance to the bombers, so [we] turned into Germans and pursued them over the Ruhr Valley. The 109s put their noses down and outran [us]." Attempting to close with the fleeing Gustavs, the Lightnings dropped their belly tanks and "in no time, we had to turn back to base, low on fuel." No losses were experienced by either side.

Having taken off from Husum again at 1245hrs, I./JG 11 – reinforced by 10. Staffel from Aalbørg – raced south, Gruppenkommandeur Hermichen leading them to catch the 2nd Combat Bombardment Wing's (CBW) now unescorted B-24s as they began releasing their bombloads over Braunschwieg. Unopposed, the reinforced Jagdgruppe shot down five Liberators – Hermichen claiming to bring down four of these in just 18 minutes. The I. and 10./JG 11 suffered no losses.

Heavy cloud cover hindered the attacks of the 2nd Bombardment Division. While the 87 Liberators (20th CBW) bombing the GWF plant at Gotha were effective, only 76 B-24s

Peggy, the P-51B-1 (43-12451) mount of 1st Lieutenant Gil Talbot of the 354th FG's 355th Fighter Squadron, having its 75-gallon drop tanks mounted in preparation for a bomber escort mission from RAF Boxted. Eventually becoming a five-victory ace, Talbot was credited with his first kill – an Me 410 – on a fighter sweep the day before Operation *Argument* began. (NMUSAF 190211-F-ZZ999-1006)

Above and beyond the call of duty, Leipzig, February 20

The 305th BG formed the 40th Combat Wing's lead combat group with its 364th BS flying – at 28,000ft – as its high squadron. Flying one of the newest B-17Gs in the group – 42-38109 "Cabin in the Sky" – 1st Lieutenant William R. "Bill" Lawley maintained formation with his leader as the wing crossed their target and unleashed their loads of 500lb GP HE and incendiary bombs. But the sub-zero temperatures at high altitude froze "Cabin in the Sky's" bomb release mechanism and its eight 500-pounders refused to fall.

As the formation rolled out of its turn off target, it was hit head-on by approximately 20 Me 109G interceptors that had raced northwards from Neubiberg, near Munich. Led by Major Walter Brede, I./JG 301's vicious frontal attack smashed the B-17's cockpit, killing the co-pilot, Lieutenant Paul Murphy, wounding Lawley and seven others, and set the number two engine ablaze.

The stricken Fortress plummeted from the formation, the wounded pilot wrestling to recover to level flight at 12,000ft through sheer strength of holding the co-pilot's body off the controls and pulling with all his might. Lawley ordered the crew to bail out but was quickly informed that two of the gunners were so severely wounded that they would not survive.

His Medal of Honor citation reads, "Because of the helpless condition of his wounded crew members 1st Lt. Lawley elected to remain with the ship and bring them to safety if it was humanly possible. Enemy fighters again attacked but by using masterful evasive action he managed to lose them. 1st Lt. Lawley remained at his post, refusing first aid until he collapsed from sheer exhaustion caused by loss of blood, shock, and the energy he had expended in keeping control of his plane. He was revived by the bombardier and again took over the controls. Coming over the English coast [one] engine started to burn and continued to do so until a successful crash landing was made on a small fighter base. Through his heroism and exceptional flying skill, 1st Lt. Lawley rendered outstanding distinguished and valorous service to our Nation."

By the time the 94th CBW arrived over Leipzig, the skies below opened up, permitting very accurate visual bombing of the Erla Me 109G factory. Badly depleted the night before by the heavy RAF raid on the city, German flak was light and inaccurate and failed to disrupt the combat wing's bomb run. (NMUSAF)

(2nd CBW) dropped on the two primary MAIG factories. The 58 Liberators (14th CBW) tasked to bomb the Halberstadt Junkers plant found their target obscured by clouds, so attempted to drop on the Messerschmitt works at Helmstedt instead – 23 others released their loads on various T/Os in the area. Overall, Hodges' division lost eight B-24s shot down – mostly from Hermichen's attack – and another three damaged beyond repair and written off as salvage upon return to England.

From overhead Bielefeld, the four combat wings composing Williams's 1st Bombardment Division's main force – reduced by air aborts to about 330 bombers at this point – turned almost due east, heading for Luckenwalde, a city 30 miles south of Berlin, while 60 B-17s of Brigadier General Robert Travis's 41st CBW angled southeast to bomb Bernburg's Junkers assembly plant.

To intercept the huge formations, acting commander Oberleutnant Rudolf Patzak's III./JG 54 Grünherz (Green Heart) was scrambled from Ludwigslust at 1212hrs, while Hauptmann Richard Lewens' I./JG 302 Wild Sau night-fighters – totaling some 50 Me 109Gs – launched from Jüterbog about the same time, augmented by Me 110 night-fighters from II./NJG 5 and II./NJG 6, while two additional Jagdgruppen were called in from 3. and 7. Jagddivision.

Colonel Harold Bowman (401st BG CO) led the 94th CBW and 1st Bomb Division's main strike force, which was intercepted by Patzak's Gefechtsverband as they passed Oschersleben. With no escorts in sight, the Me 109G formations broke up to conduct Schwarm (four-aeroplane formation) and individual firing passes, damaging several Fortresses. Fortunately, Patzak's attacks were interrupted by the timely arrival of IX Fighter Command's 354th FG, led by Lieutenant Colonel George R. "Uncle" Bickell (CO 355th FS). Leading 54 Mustangs, Bickell found the bombers under attack and engaged immediately. Busy with their attacks on the bombers, the Messerschmitts were overwhelmed by the Mustangs – III./JG 54 lost eight Me 109Gs and three pilots, I./JG 302 lost five Gustavs with two pilots wounded, and the two Me 110G units lost two aircraft and four aircrew. The 354th FG lost no P-51s in these battles.

At Luckenwalde, Bowman's four combat wings turned south, then southwest to begin their bomb runs on the four targets clustered around Leipzig. Approaching the city, the bombers were attacked by Major Rudolf-Emil Schnoor's I./JG 1. Having taken off from Dortmund at 1300hrs, they pursued the Fortress formations deep into Germany – flying a long tail chase – until Bowman turned his strike force back to attack their targets. Fighting their way through Bickell's Mustangs, Schnoor's Fw 190As shot down one 381st BG B-17F but lost three Focke-Wulfs, with two pilots killed and the third wounded.

Leading the attack on Leipzig, Colonel Bowman later reported, "As we approached the target area, the clouds opened up to 'scattered' and a visual sighting was made. The result was, for our group, 100 per cent of our bombs were within one thousand feet of the aiming point. Hits were made on the principal assembly shop of the Erla Messerschmitt production factory [at Mockau], and its other large assembly building was observed to be on fire as the other bombers left the target area."

As the Fortresses made their bomb runs, they were subjected to fierce head-on attacks by Major Walter Brede's I./JG 301 Wild Sau night-interceptors. Called in from Generalleutnant Joachim-Friedrich Huth's semi-autonomous 7. Jagddivision, Brede's 20 Me 109Gs took off from Munich's Neubiberg airfield around 1300hrs and raced north at high altitude. Brede's Gustavs shot one 401st BG Fortress out of formation (it crashed near Magdeburg while attempting to escape to Sweden) and damaged two others so badly they crash-landed upon return. These two – one from the 305th BG, the other from the 351st BG – made it back to England only through the most heroic personal efforts, resulting in three awards of the Medal of Honor (MOH) for courageous and sacrificial actions "above and beyond the call of duty."

As Bowman's strike force began egressing the target area, the Eighth's 357th FG – flying its first bomber escort mission – arrived. Led by Lieutenant Colonel Donald Blakeslee (4th FG CO), a highly experienced fighter leader with ten confirmed aerial victories, the 357th FG's 19 P-51s arrived on time (1356hrs) at 25,000ft but found that the last interceptors had headed to their bases. Sweeping through the target area, Blakeslee turned west to clear the bombers' egress route and encountered a small formation of Me 109Gs and several individual Gustavs. Two were shot down, but one Mustang was damaged over Leipzig, forcing the pilot to bail out and become a prisoner of war (POW).

Low on fuel, the 354th and 357th FGs headed back to their bases in England, leaving the returning bombers unprotected until they could be joined by their withdrawal support fighters. To minimize their exposure to Schmid's interceptors, the American bombers initially turned southwest and flew a circuitous routing back across Belgium. This completely fooled the Luftwaffe fighter controllers, who expected that – as had typically been the case in the past – the bombers would simply reverse course and fly directly back to England. In anticipation of this, they had landed their interceptors to refuel and rearm at airfields along the expected return routing.

Meanwhile, Lützow sent five Nachtjagdgruppen after the now unescorted bomber formations, hoping to destroy some of the many stragglers as they egressed from the target area. Scrambling from Hildesheim as soon as his Hornissen were refueled and rearmed, Tratt led II./ZG 26 in an intercept near Meiningen (southwest of Gotha) that claimed two more Fortresses shot down (neither were credited) in exchange for two Me 410s lost. Other units included I./NJG 6 and I. and III./ZG 76, who shot down three lagging battle-damaged Fortresses (from 92nd, 305th, and 306th BGs) and one Liberator (44th BG; claimed as a B-17) for three Me 110Gs lost. Last to engage, 20 Me 110Gs from I./ZG 26 intercepted the B-17s south of Koblenz at 1445–1450hrs but very quickly suffered grievously at the hands of arriving Thunderbolts.

About the same time, Major Walther Dahl's III./JG 3 joined the battle. Launched from Leipheim in Bavaria at about 1300hrs, Dahl's pilots shot down one 445th BG B-24H northeast of Koblenz just before the withdrawal support Thunderbolts arrived. III./JG 3 lost five Gustavs destroyed, with two pilots killed and a third wounded.

One of the first withdrawal support units to arrive was Colonel Joe Mason's 352nd FG, which rendezvoused with the retiring bombers near Koblenz, and while "the 328th FS fought a running battle across the entire withdrawal route," the 486th FS "intercepted a gaggle of fighters in the rendezvous area," resulting in two extended engagements. A total of 11 kills were claimed, seven of them the hapless Me 110 Zerstörers (I./ZG 26 actually lost six) claimed by the 328th FS, and the rest were probably Dahl's Gustavs and three Volkel-based

1st Lieutenant William Lawley was awarded the Medal of Honor for his heroic actions under fire. (USAF Photo 160510-D-LN615-006)

An attacking P-47 films his flight leader shooting down an Me 110G, one of 18 lost on the opening day of Operation *Argument*. It was another bad day for the Luftwaffe's *Zerstörer* force, and it wasn't going to get any better. (NMUSAF)

Major Oskar-Heinz (Heinrich) "Pritzl" Bär. Bär was a very popular, highly experienced combat leader with 183 victories to his credit, who had been demoted by Göring to a mere *Staffelkapitän* (squadron commander) due to his disagreements with various elements of Luftwaffe leadership. Leading 6./JG 1, Bär was credited with two B-17s and a P-51 shot down this day. (Author's Collection)

Me 109Gs (III./JG 1 and I./JG 3) claimed destroyed over Nivelles and near Charleroi. The 352nd FG lost no P-47s in these combats.

The famous, high-scoring 4th FG – the RAF's former Eagle Squadrons now had 150 victories to their credit – flew to Kirchberg, and at 1429hrs rendezvoused with the main strike force northeast of Koblenz at 23,000ft. They found five Messerschmitts firing rockets into the withdrawing bomber formations, and the 335th FS promptly claimed two Me 110s shot down. One 335th Thunderbolt was lost to a pair of IV./JG 3 Me 109Gs (reported as Fw 190s), and the pilot killed, just after he and his flight leader claimed a third Me 110 downed near Aachen.

Major Wilhelm Gäth's II./JG 26 took off from several Dutch airfields at about 1430hrs to engage the straggling bombers. Two Schwarme joined up over southeast Belgium, and while attacking one of the trailing combat wings near Malmedy, the eight Fw 190s were jumped by 4th FG Thunderbolts. One Focke-Wulf was shot down – the pilot bailed out with minor injuries – and three others damaged.

From Cormeilles in France, Generalmajor Karl Hentschel's 5. Jagddivision sent III./JG 2 to intercept the retiring bombers over Belgium. They shot down one straggling B-24J west of Charleroi and, at 1516hrs, Gruppenkommandeur Hauptmann Herbert Huppertz shot down a 91st BG B-17F over Mons. Engaged by 355th FG Thunderbolts, Huppertz's unit lost two Fw 190s shot down with one pilot killed. The last home-bound bombers crossed the Channel coast 32 minutes later.

This last "kill claim" ended a very frustrating day for the Luftwaffe – and a significant victory for the Americans. The Eighth AF had performed brilliantly where the weather permitted. While the 3rd Bomb Division's mission was ineffective due to clouds covering the targets and the 2nd Bomb Division's strikes on the Braunschwieg factories were only partially successful, the Gotha Me 110G factory was heavily damaged.

Of 417 B-17s dispatched to attack targets at Leipzig and Bernburg, 276 bombed their primary targets. Three of the four targets at Leipzig were bombed by 239 B-17s, destroying 74 percent of the ATG/Erla-Maschinenwerke complex. At the Mockau Me 109G assembly plant, 83 percent of the floor space was destroyed, while at Heiterblick, 65 percent of the factory was destroyed. Abtnaundorf was only lightly damaged and Aschersleben was missed altogether. Some 160 new Me 109Gs were damaged or destroyed on the ground, and the resulting production stoppage and delays cost another 350 Me 109s.

At Bernburg, only one of the 41st CBW's two BGs was able to get "lined up" on the target during their bomb run (the other dropped on Helmstedt instead), resulting in just 37 B-17s (384th BG) attacking the Bernburg Ju 88/188 assembly plant. Consequently, the resulting damage was only moderate – this target would have to be struck again.

The cost had been surprisingly low. The Eighth AF's fighter escorts proved so effective that the 1st and 2nd Bombardment Divisions had lost only 15 bombers shot down, with five more written off to salvage. In personnel losses, 149 aircrewmen had been killed or were missing, and another 27 crewmen returned wounded.

By every measure, the RLV had suffered a sharp defeat. The I. Jagdkorps reported, "Weather conditions precluded the assembling of our aircraft into large closed formations. Some of our smaller formations succeeded in contacting the enemy and became involved in heavy combat with American fighter aircraft. The casualty rate was very high." The command had launched

362 fighters, including night-fighters, but only 155 engaged the enemy in combat. Of these, 75 were lost, representing a 20.7 percent loss rate.

While the Luftwaffe HQ's Quartermaster (OKL's 4. Abteilung, the supply directorate) recorded the loss of 54 aircraft written off (destroyed or assessed as 60 per cent or more damaged) in the West – Luftflotte Reich and Luftflotte 3 combined – a much closer examination of unit records by historian Donald Caldwell reveals that the Luftwaffe lost a total of 74 aircraft. This included 42 day-fighters (38 Me 109Gs and four Fw 190s), 20 Zerstörers (18 Me 110Gs and two Me 410s), and a dozen Wild Sau single-engine night-fighters (Me 109Gs).

Germany's fighter production rate at the time could easily replace these losses, but trained pilots and aircrew were already in short supply. Caldwell's study also revealed that the Luftwaffe lost 13 single-engine fighter pilots and 24 twin-engine aircrew members killed, along with six Wild Sau pilots. Another 29 were wounded or injured in accidents and would not be available to fly the next day.

Overall, German single-engine fighter pilot losses were not heavy but, compared with the VIII FC's loss of three fighter pilots missing in action, meant that the Luftwaffe was losing over six single-engine fighter pilots (19 in total) for each American fighter pilot who did not return from the missions that day. It was attrition warfare at its grimmest, and the Americans had won the first battle of the campaign.

A Fw 190A under attack by an Eighth AF escort fighter. (USAF Photo)

Eighth AF Mission 228, February 21

The next night, RAF Bomber Command struck Stuttgart – home to the Bosch Aktiengesellschaft (AG), making aeroengine magnetos and other aircraft accessories; the huge Daimler-Benz AG, making the supercharged V12 engines powering Me 109Gs, 110Gs, and 410s; and the Swedish-owned SKF anti-friction bearings factories – with 527 Lancasters and Halifaxes. The city was blanketed with thick clouds, the H2S radar-released bombs plummeting through the undercast to damage the Bad Cannstatt and Feuerbach districts, killing 160 civilians and injuring another 977. Losses were light – seven Lancasters and one Halifax – thanks to 228 other British bombers flying two diversionary flights over the North Sea and to Munich two hours beforehand and the thick ice-laden weather spread across southern Germany.

For USSTAF planning purposes, it was hoped that the raid would result in I. Jagdkorps anticipating another Eighth AF attack on the same target – as happened the night and day before – and repositioning its outlying interceptor units deeper into Germany while Doolittle's heavy bombers struck shorter-ranged targets in northeastern Germany. Having temporarily throttled fighter production at Leipzig, Bernburg, and Gotha, Anderson's next wave of attacks was intended to devastate the Diepholz depot and five large airfields where newly produced aircraft had been seen parked in open storage, thus eliminating numerous replacement aircraft in the supply chain. To that end, Williams' 1st Bomb Division targeted Gütersloh, Lippstadt, and Werf southeast of Bielefeld, and Hodge's 2nd BD was sent to hit Achmer, near Osnabrück, and Münster-Handorf airfields. Not pleased with the previous day's results at Braunschweig, Anderson sent LeMay's 3rd Bombardment Division to hit the two MAIG factories there and the large Luftwaffe air depot at Fliegerhorst Diepholz.

Shown here inspecting JG 2 in April 1942, Generalmajor Max-Josef Ibel was a career fighter pilot with outstanding leadership credentials, having been a Staffelkapitän, Gruppekommandeur, and Geschwaderkommodore in the pre-war Luftwaffe. He commanded JG 27 during the Battle of Britain and later became Jafü 3, directing fighter operations from France, before taking command of 2. Jagddivision in October 1943. (Author's Collection)

A total of 617 Fortresses and 244 Liberators were dispatched. These were escorted by 542 Thunderbolts (13 FGs) providing penetration and withdrawal support, with 69 Lightnings and 68 Mustangs assigned to cover the bombers in the target area. While it was expected that bad weather would disrupt most bombing attacks, at the end of the day Anderson said, "The reason for the operation today was to shoot down enemy fighters as much as possible and we did not expect to be able to see many [of the] targets."

Not surprisingly, the Ninth AF's planned airfield suppression raids against Luftwaffe bases in the Low Countries were largely aborted due to the expansive undercast. The exception was the 322nd BG's attack on Koksijde-Veurne airfield (near Dunkirk) in Belgium. Led by an AN/APS-15-equipped B-26 from the 1st Pathfinder Squadron (Provisional), 17 Marauders dropped their bombloads through the clouds, hitting the abandoned airfield.

Spearheading the 860 heavies, flying in a long stream of 15 combat wings, were 281 of LeMay's 3rd Bomb Division B-17s headed for Diepholz and Braunschweig. Knowing the weather would probably limit opportunities for visual bombing, Anderson had LeMay's combat wings led by the 482nd BG Pathfinders. Normally the Eighth AF's radar development and training unit assigned to the second-line Composite Command, the bombardiers would release their bombloads using AN/APS-15 "blind bombing" radar and the Fortresses following them would drop on their signal.

Once again, the Americans' bomber stream was initially arrowing straight for Berlin, with Williams' Fortresses and Hodge's Liberators following LeMay's, their long flanks covered by six Thunderbolt fighter groups. The leading combat wings were detected by 3. Jagddivision's coastal EW radars about noon, and bombers began crossing the Dutch coast between The Hague and Den Helder at 1222hrs. Eight minutes later, Grabmann responded by scrambling five Fw 190A and Me 109G Jagdgruppen (all of JG 1 and I. and IV./JG 3) and one Me 110 shadower, which was quickly shot down by an escorting 56th FG P-47. Ibel launched ten Me 110G Zerstörers (III./ZG 26) to break up the bomber formations, to be reinforced by two Zerstörergruppen (I. and II./ZG 76) and one of the Wild Sau interceptors (I./JG 301) flying north from Huth's 7. Jagddivision. Dutch and Belgian airfields were all "socked in" by low, wet ceilings (600–1,500ft), and JG 26 could only move its fighters to locations with better weather and await the return of the bomber stream.

The thick heavy weather and poor instrument proficiency of the Jagdwaffe pilots required them to penetrate the clouds individually or in small sections, hoping to rendezvous into larger formations "on top," but the ice-laden clouds extended up to an altitude of 5,000ft. Although visibility above was excellent (30–50 miles), the impenetrable cloud layer spread the climbing interceptors widely, precluding forming their Gefechtsverbände formations.

The largest was Hauptmann Hermann Seegatz's II./JG 1, which launched 24 Fw 190As from Rheine at 1245hrs. As Seegatz gathered most of his interceptors and they began their long laborious climbs to 26,000ft to meet the approaching bombers, Lieutenant Colonel Donald Blakeslee's 4th FG rendezvoused with the three combat wings headed for Braunschweig. At 1340hrs, 15 of Seegatz's Fw 190s were sighted 11,000ft below and were attacked by the 334th FS, who scattered the formation and claimed two shot down – the unit actually lost four fighters, with two pilots killed and another two wounded. Blakeslee's Thunderbolts suffered no losses.

Despite these losses, JG 1 was able to shoot down one 457th BG B-17G over Dümmer Lake and damaged another so badly it was credited to Major Oskar-Heinz "Pritzl" Bär as a Herausschüss (literally "shooting out" – damaging a bomber so badly it fell out of formation and became a straggler). Additionally, JG 3's two Gruppen claimed only a single Herausschüss but lost four Me 109Gs – possibly to the 355th and 356th FGs, which claimed the same number of victories in exchange for one 356th Thunderbolt shot down by Gustavs over Bad Münder, killing the pilot.

Just after 1300hrs, Ibel launched his main interceptor force – four Jagdgruppen (all of JG 11 and II./JG 3) – while Lützow scrambled one group of Me 109Gs (III./JG 54) and two Zerstörergruppen (I. and II./ZG 26) to reinforce 2. Jagddivision's first responders. An estimated 200 interceptors began converging on the 3rd Bomb Division's leading combat wings just as the last penetration support P-47 groups, low on fuel, turned back for England.

Meanwhile, approaching Diepholz, two combat wings sheered away from the main force and – finding the large fighter air depot lying totally exposed in a wide area clear of clouds – delivered a devastatingly accurate bombing attack.

The other three combat wings continued on to Braunschweig, where they found the city blanketed by an expansive undercast and most BGs reverted to radar-directed blind bombing, releasing their loads on the signal from the 482nd BG Pathfinders. Explosions rocked through the city but only one of the two MIAG factories was damaged. Brigadier General Russell Wilson's 4th CBW turned around and found the city of Hannover in the clear, and 88 B-17s bombed that city. Others saved their loads for Diepholz and added to the destruction there during their return flight.

Led by MOH-winner and five-victory ace Lieutenant Colonel James "Big Jim" Howard, the three dozen Mustangs of the 354th FG arrived as the bombers passed Diepholz and found the Braunschweig strike force under persistent attacks that shot down one 96th BG B-17G over the city and damaged another from 100th BG so badly it crash-landed in Holland during its return flight. Engaging immediately, nine victories were claimed in the running fight to Braunschweig – II./JG 11 lost one Me 109G, II./JG 3 lost two, and III./JG 54 lost four more, with five pilots being killed. Two 354th FG Mustangs were lost in these combats; one pilot perished and the other was captured.

Colonel Henry Spicer's 357th FG were also involved, shooting down one Me 109G, the debris from which disabled the attacking P-51B, forcing the pilot to bail out to become a POW. Most importantly, the escorts prevented many of the interceptors from attacking the B-17s, limiting the 3rd Bomb Division's combat losses to only two in the target area.

Passing Meppen, Williams' 1st Bomb Division turned southeast towards the Dortmund–Bielefeld region and Hodge's B-24s angled for the Münster–Osnabrück area, but four of the five airfield targets were completely obscured by thick clouds. Lacking pathfinders or radar-bombing equipment, the combat wings separated into individual BGs and began milling around the area, their bombardiers visually searching for something worthwhile to bomb. Lieutenant Colonel William Buck, leading the 41st CBW, called it a "scavenger hunt."

The 44th BG Liberators – the Flying Eightballs – obliterating the Deipholz Air Depot. (NMUSAF 180422-F-FN604-033)

Colonel Hubert Zemke, CO of 56th FG, getting strapped into the cockpit of his P-47D Thunderbolt prior to leading another fighter escort mission from RAF Manston. (USAF Photo)

Just north-northwest of Osnabrück, 11 B-24s (93rd BG, out of 32 in total) bombed Achmer – the only airfield target seen – followed by three groups of 1st Bomb Division Fortresses (91st, 351st, and 381st BGs). Attacked by Hauptmann "Toni" Hackl's III./JG 11, the 91st BG lost two B-17Fs and one B-17G, resulting in seven crewmen killed and 23 POWs.

Near Hesepe airfield, the 448th BG's Liberators were attacked by Hauptmann Kurd Peters' Wild Sau Fw 190As (II./JG 300), who shot down two of them. Major Walter Brede's I./JG 301 engaged one of the many wandering bomber formations but, according to the official history, "the Wild Sau pilots had yet to discover the proper tactics for attacking formation of bombers, so this mission was an unsuccessful one for the Gruppe." No victories could be claimed and two Me 109Gs were lost.

Meanwhile, as on the previous day, the Zerstörers suffered grievously, ZG 26 and ZG 76 each losing three Me 110Gs – with a total of nine aircrew killed – without shooting down a single American bomber. Tratt's II./ZG 26 was the only successful unit, 4. Staffel's *Unteroffizier* (Uffz, or Corporal) Adolf Wenzel being credited with two 92nd BG Fortresses shot down southeast of Bielefeld between 1400 and 1405hrs, the second one resulting from a fatal ramming attack that brought down B-17G 42-31411 "Wilder-N-Hell" – killing eight crew with two captured – and his own Me 410.

While most BGs dropped their bombloads on anything that looked militarily useful – six airfields and two railways marshaling yards – one group of B-24s (44th BG) and another of B-17s (303rd BG) flew to Diepholz to add their bombloads to the air depot's mounting destruction. Major Walter Shayler, leading the 360th BS Fortresses, reported, "We sure hit something at this aerodrome. There was a horrible mess of smoke and flames coming up. Somebody was there before us, so we just added a bit to the general damage."

As the many disorganized bomber formations headed west once again, additional interceptors – and some units that had landed and were quickly refueled and rearmed – were launched from 1415–1447hrs.

The first of these were five FW 190As from Bär's 6./JG 1. At 1525hrs, he shot down the 91st BG B-17F 42-3040 "Miss Ouachita" north-northwest of Rheine airfield during the 1st Bomb Division's return to England; it crash-landed just short of the Dutch border with two crewmen killed and eight taken prisoner. Additionally, during their return the 92nd BG lost one B-17G that crashed just off-shore at Ostend in Belgium, and the 351st lost a B-17F that ditched 20 miles off Lowestoft.

Taking off from Langenhagen at 1430hrs, six heavily armed and thickly armored Fw 190A-7/R2 Sturmjäger ('Shock Fighter', similar to the army's Sturmtruppen or "shock" assault troops) of Sturmstaffel 1 claimed to have shot down two Flying Fortresses and a third Herausschüss. Pressing their stern attacks to extremely close quarters – and ramming if necessary – the elite squadron lost two shock fighters to the Boeings' withering rear quarter defensive fire, both of them crashing near Lübbecke, north of Bielefeld, killing both pilots.

Sent to provide withdrawal support, according to Luftwaffe records, "A fighter force, crossing the coast between 1325 and 1400, picked up the returning bombers over Osnabrück and accompanied them back to their home bases."

The most successful of the arriving Thunderbolt groups was Colonel Hubert "Hub" Zemke's 56th FG, the unit's second mission of the day being led by Major Leroy Schreiber (62nd FS Operations Officer). In a wild series of clashes that defy coherent description, Schreiber's three squadrons claimed 11 enemy fighters destroyed. Most of these were probably from Hauptmann Friedrich Eberle's III./JG 1 which launched from Volkel at 1415hrs – they lost six Me 109Gs, with three pilots killed and a fourth wounded. No 56th FG Thunderbolts were lost.

Zemke later stated, "Enemy formations were showing a marked lack of coordination. We did not know it then but this was often due to pilots refueling away from home base and joining with others from different units for second sorties against the bombers."

Making contrails high above the North Sea, the unescorted 92nd Bomb Group flies in a loose combat wing heading to Denmark, high above an expansive undercast, as a diversion for the day's main effort. (NARA)

Last to launch this day was Major Wilhelm Gäth's II./JG 26, taking off from Melsbroek, Belgium, at 1525hrs to harry the last retiring bombers as they approached the coast. Over the IJsselmeer, nine Fw 190As (5./JG 26) intercepted the retiring 95th BG at 1550hrs and shot down one B-17F; it crashed into the sea 2 miles off Egmond, Holland. Fifteen minutes later, another flight (7./JG 26) shot down another 95th BG straggler just northwest of Utrecht.

Overall, it was a disappointing day for both sides.

Doolittle's command had lost 17 bombers in combat. Williams' 1st Bomb Division suffered the most, losing eight Fortresses shot down by fighters and another (457th BG) so severely damaged it was written off as salvage after landing at RAF Glatton. Hodge's 2nd Bomb Division lost only two 448th BG Liberators over Germany, a third (392nd BG) crashed into the North Sea, and a fourth (448th BG) was written off as salvage upon return to RAF Seething. LeMay's 3rd Bomb Division lost five Fortresses in combat, three of them over Holland during their return to base (RTB), including a 482nd BG Pathfinder over the IJsselmeer.

The expansive cloud cover prevented most of the planned bombing attacks, with only Diepholz being effectively struck. With double the planned number of bombers pounding this hapless air depot, Anderson proudly reported that Diepholz was "severely and accurately bombed."

The bad weather also limited I. Jagdkorps' response, with only 282 sorties launched, of which approximately half actually engaged the bombers milling around northwestern Germany. Additionally, the thick clouds prevented the responding interceptors from organizing their massed set-piece Gefechtsverbände attacks. The smaller, scattered formations had to resort to quick hit-and-run engagements – drastically reducing the numbers of bombers claimed but increasing the attackers' survivability in the face of the now ever-present fighter escorts.

Just as the weather restricted the I. Jagdkorps' response, the smaller numbers of interceptors airborne reduced the numbers of Luftwaffe fighters Eighth AF fighter groups destroyed to less than half that of the day before. OKL's Quartermaster recorded the loss of 29 aircraft written off the inventory of Luftflotte Reich and Luftflotte 3. Donald Caldwell's extensive research confirms the loss of 34 aircraft: 20 Me 109Gs, seven Fw 190As, six Me 110Gs, and one Me 410. Fourteen single-engine fighter pilots and ten twin-engine aircrew were killed.

Kepner's VIII FC lost five fighter-pilots missing in action. In addition to the Mustang lost due to damage from an exploding Messerschmitt, two Thunderbolts failed to return, one of which crash-landed in Holland with engine failure, the pilot evading capture to eventually return to the UK. The resulting aircrew "kill ratio" – about 5:1 – remained about the same as the day before.

Eighth AF Mission 230, February 22

Despite the previous day's disappointments – caused almost completely by the pervasive adverse weather – February 22 promised better prospects as the Baltic high pressure system moved southwards across eastern Germany, bringing clear skies to Bavaria. This allowed strikes to be planned against two of the Eighth AF's top-priority – and most dreaded – targets: the large Messerschmitt manufacturing complexes at Regensburg and the ball-bearing producing factories at Schweinfurt.

Released from its tactical, army-support operations in Italy, Twining's Fifteenth AF was directed to attack the former while Doolittle dispatched LeMay's 3rd Bombardment Division against the latter. Approaching the two closely spaced targets from opposite directions, it was hoped that the Eighth AF's much larger striking force (a planned 360 B-17s) would attract Luftflotte Reich's attention sufficiently to allow Twining's 204 bombers to reach their target with little opposition.

To help the 3rd Bomb Division get to its target, LeMay's five combat wings would penetrate the Reich's airspace in train with Hodges' Liberators and Williams' 1st Bomb Division. Knowing that persistent attacks against the same targets was fundamental to success, Anderson sent Hodges' 180 B-24s to once again bomb the Me 110G factories at Gotha. Leaving the main body en route, Williams' strike force – five combat wings totaling about 300 B-17s – would fan out to hit individual targets. Two would strike the AGO (Apparatebau GmbH Oschersleben) Flugzeugwerke's Fw 190 factory, now the largest producer of the Focke-Wulf fighter after the devastation of Marienburg, and the Ju 188 fuselage manufacturer at Oscherleben. Three others would be hitting other Ju 88/188 component factories and assembly plants at Aschersleben, Bernburg, and Halberstadt.

Flying a feint across the North Sea to Aalborg, Denmark, Brigadier General Howard Turner's 40th CBW organized a 41-bomber combat wing from the 92nd and 305th BGs. Aboard the former were newly developed GM-Delco APT-3 Mandrel that broadcast 125MHz noise-jamming against the Luftwaffe's Freya, Mammut and Wassermann EW radars to "make it hard for the enemy to detect the main force of bombers until it had formed over England." Additionally, the Ninth AF dispatched 177 B-26 Marauders to bomb two Dutch airfields and pave the way for the main striking force.

At 0815hrs, the Funkaufklärungsdienst informed Schmid and his I. Jagdkorps staff that large American formations were assembling over eastern England. This proved to be one of the most difficult parts of the day's mission.

While skies were clear over Bavaria, thick ice-filled clouds were solid up to 24,000ft over East Anglia, preventing many of LeMay's formations from assembling and causing several mid-air collisions, one claiming 18 lives. Finally, in frustration, LeMay ordered his division to abort the mission and return to base. Meanwhile, at much lower altitudes, Ninth AF's B-26s began crossing the coast at 1010hrs. The 98th Bomb Wing (323rd and 389th BGs) aborted due to heavy cloud and reduced visibility underneath. Sixty-six Marauders (322nd and 386th BGs) dropped 89 tons of bombs on Gilze-Rijen but lost two B-26s to AA fire (Flak Abt 932). The target was home to NJG 3's Ju 88C night-fighters, but no appreciable damage was done.

Flying 60–100 miles off the Dutch and German North Sea coast, the Mandrel jammers proved ineffective – their 100Watt transmitting power was insufficient to overcome the great distance – and the Luftwaffe EW radars detected the main force at 1118hrs, crossing the Dutch coast between Katwijk and the mouth of the Scheldt some 21 minutes later.

The previous day, Schmid had issued new operations orders, emphasizing the need to intercept the incoming raiders as far out as possible. Now that Eighth AF bombers were being escorted all the way to targets deep in Germany, it made little sense to delay interception until the escorting fighters turned for home. This decision brought Luftflotte 3's interceptors into the battle in full strength.

As the Americans' main strike force was detected, Grabmann called for support from Sperrle's fighters and the two Luftflotte 3 Jagddivisionen launched about 60 Fw 190As to engage over Holland. Generalmajor Karl Hentschel's 5. Jagddivision scrambled two Gruppen (II. and III./JG 2) from Cormeilles-en-Vexin and Creil in France at 1115hrs; ten and 20 minutes later, Oberst Carl Vieck launched two more (I. and II./JG 26) from Florennes in Belgium and Laon-Athies, respectively. From his own forces, Grabmann launched 21 Fw 190As (II./JG 1) from Rheine at 1125hrs.

Unable to assemble over England due to the solid cloud cover at higher altitudes, 255 B-17s headed east more or less on schedule – dictated by the rendezvous timings with the escorting fighter groups – attempting to join together in their bomb groups and combat wings along the way. Separated from their units, many individual and small formations of Fortresses abandoned the mission and returned to their bases, resulting in only 187 flying effective missions.

For example, the 1st CBW's 381st BG could collect only 12 out of the 31 B-17s launched, these joining with 15 (of 32) from 91st BG to form a very small combat wing headed for Oschersleben to bomb the AGO Focke-Wulf factory. Having taken too long to collect 27 bombers, Brigadier General William Gross's 1st CBW headed across Holland without ever seeing any of their scheduled penetration escorts. This formation was followed by a composite combat wing composed primarily of the 401st BG, which was assigned to attack the Ju 188 fuselage factory at Oscherleben.

Likewise, Hodge's Liberators also headed east hoping to form into combat wings en route. However, assembling the widely dispersed and badly strung out groups into larger, more defensible formations proved impossible and, learning that LeMay's 333 Flying Fortresses had abandoned the mission, Hodges recalled his 177 Liberators when the leading elements were about 100 miles inland. During their return flight, 74 B-24s attempted to bomb four Luftwaffe airfields in Holland. However, none of these were being used by Grabmann's 3. Jagddivision and no particular damage was done anyway, rendering the mission completely ineffective.

As the disorganized ingress – and the Liberators' disorderly return – progressed, the first of six P-47 penetration support fighter groups began arriving, looking for their charges, but the disarray of the bomber formations precluded effective escort. Taking advantage of the muddle, Hauptmann Herbert Huppertz's III./JG 2 successfully intercepted Hodge's returning B-24s. As he was shooting down a 44th BG bomber at 1220hrs during a running battle from Helmond to Breda, Huppertz was himself shot down and wounded. The 2nd Bombardment Division lost three Liberators on this aborted mission – two from the 44th BG and the third from the 453rd BG.

An estimated dozen Fw 190s from Hauptmann Karl Borris' I./JG 26 intercepted one formation of B-17s north of Eindhoven at 1223hrs, but were themselves engaged by the P-47s of Colonel Tom Christian's 361st FG. One Thunderbolt was shot down – with the pilot killed – without loss to the Focke-Wulfs. The resulting melee stripped away the escorting fighters, allowing Major Wilhelm Gäth's II./JG 26 and Hauptmann Kurt Buhligen's II./JG 2 to intercept Travis's 41st CBW combat wing approaching the Dutch–German border at about 1245hrs. "They were on us before we knew it," reported Major George Harris (CO 546th BS). "They came at us out of the sun and we couldn't see them until they were right in our formation. The sun was bright and it was clear as hell. They gave us the works. They came at us a dozen at a time, then they would wheel around and attack us from the rear."

Gäth's Focke-Wulf pilots shot down three 384th BG B-17Gs between Venlay in Holland and Wesel in Germany. A 384th BG B-17F was shot down further east, near Dorsten, by the *Staffelkapitän* (Staka, or squadron commander) of 5./JG 26, Oberfeldwebel Adolf "Addi" Glunz, to become his 55th victory. Meanwhile, Buhligen's Gustav pilots damaged a 303rd BG Fortress so badly it crash-landed 20 miles southwest of Utrecht, six of its crew luckily evading capture.

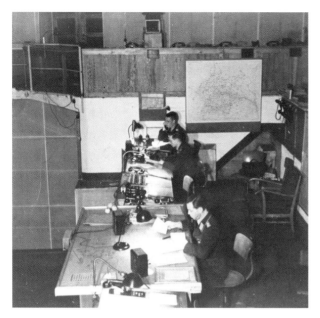

Fighter control officers (JLOs) at the 2. Jagddivision's Gefechtsstand From this *Jägerleitpulten* (fighter control position), responding fighter units were directed to intercept incoming bomber tracks, their instructions being radioed to airborne interceptor leaders by GCI controllers seated in front of the Jägerleitpulten. (Bundesarchiv, Bild 141-1341, Fotograf(in): o.Ang.)

OPPOSITE
Designed to operate from the Kriegsmarine's unfinished aircraft carrier *Graf Zeppelin*, the old, obsolescent Bf 109T had been withdrawn from front-line combat because its very light armament of only two small 7.92mm MG 17 machine guns and a pair of MG FF 20mm cannon made it unsuitable for engaging American heavy bombers or their escort fighters. For convoy protection missions in the Danish Skagerrak, 20 examples were assigned to Oberleutnant Herbert Christmann's 11./JG 11 based at Lister, Norway. (Author's Collection)

As Gäth's Fw 190s – low on fuel and out of ammunition – recovered individually to various bases, at 1250hrs, Hauptmann Hermann Seegatz's II./JG 1 began attacking the 401st BG formation north of Duisburg, damaging one Fortress so badly it eventually crashed east of Paderborn.

Meanwhile, approaching from the west was the 56th FG's A Group led by Lieutenant Colonel "Gabby" Gabreski. From overhead Arnhem in the Netherlands at 1305hrs, "a huge explosion was seen ahead in the area around the first box of bombers" as a 379th BG B-17F blew up after being hit by flak over Münster. At full throttle, the Thunderbolts overtook the leading bomber formation and found an estimated 15 Fw 190s wheeling around in a gentle left turn to fly out ahead of the bombers again and make another pass. This conveniently placed Gabreski's Thunderbolts at their vulnerable six o'clock position. The P-47s closed, Gabby shooting down one near Lippstadt and scattering the rest. Diving away could not save them, and Seegatz's II./JG 1 lost five interceptors, with one pilot wounded. The 56th FG lost no Thunderbolts.

Grabmann scrambled his main force at 1215hrs: Oberst Walter "Gulle" Oesau's Stab and I./JG 1 from Dortmund, I./JG 3 from Volkel, IV./JG 3 from Venlo, and eight Fw 190A-7 Sturmjäger from Langenhagen. These units claimed to shoot down five Fortresses – one of them claimed by Oesau over the Münster–Bielefeld area at 1336hrs for his 120th victory – with a sixth Herausschüss. In these attacks, Hauptmann Rudolf-Emil Schnoor's I./JG 1 lost three Focke-Wulfs shot down and one pilot killed, 1./JG 3 Staka and 36-victory ace Oberleutnant Ernst-Heinz Löhr. These losses were probably to the 56th FG, which claimed 15 kills for the day.

Arriving at their rendezvous near Hamm at 1303hrs, Colonel Avelin Tacon's 359th FG also witnessed the 379th BG Fortress explode and, as they closed to investigate, two minutes later the 370th FS was attacked by ten Gustavs, probably from Hauptmann Josef Haiböck's I./JG 3. The attack resulted in a swirling dogfight that spiraled down to lower altitudes with no losses suffered by either side. Seven minutes later, at 1312hrs, the 368th FS spotted three Me 109Gs attacking an aborting B-17G and dived to attack, claiming all three destroyed – these were possibly from Hauptmann Heinz Lang's IV./JG 3, which reported losing three Messerschmitts and one pilot while claiming the B-17 shot down. The crippled Fortress crashed near Afferden, Holland, at 1315hrs, with six crewmen successfully evading capture.

Meanwhile, approaching Denmark, the feint attack's 30 remaining B-17Gs found the clouds blanketing the Jutland peninsula. Lieutenant Colonel William Reid's formation had been detected by Grabmann's coastal EW radars and their progress was tracked across the North Sea. Schmid's operations officers "properly identified [this as] a small diversionary force" and passed intercept responsibility to Ibel's 2. Jagddivision, which passed interception control to Major Müller-Rendsberg at Jagdschnittsführer-Dänemark at Grove airfield (now Karup RDAF base).

Müller-Rendsberg's small force – IV./JG 11 and IV./NJG 3 – could handle one Pulk of raiders, allowing Ibel to send the rest of JG 11 south to join the main battle. From Grove, 10./NJG 3 was scrambled at 1255hrs, followed immediately by 10./JG 11's Fw 190As from Aalborg and 11./JG 11's obsolescent Bf 109Ts (or Toni, for *Trägerjäger* or carrier fighter) from Lister, Norway.

Oberleutnant Herbert Christmann's 11./JG 11 scrambled six Tonis to join 10. Staffel's Fw 190As over Grove while 10./NJG 3's Ju 88C Zerstörers ranged out over the sea to intercept Reid's formation at 1327hrs, shooting down one 92nd BG Fortress. Arriving over the target area at 1413 hrs, Reid found the airfield covered by clouds and to avoid harming Danish civilians ordered his formation to return to England with their bombs. While heading back across Jutland, the 92nd BG lost a second B-17G, reportedly to radar-directed flak.

Müller-Rendsberg's single-engined interceptors began their attacks at 1450hrs, as the bombers headed back out to sea. In repeated firing passes against the 305th BG, Christmann's pilots shot down one B-17G and damaged another so badly it crashed at Sheffield in northern England, both victims being lost with all aboard. Two of the lightly armed Tonis were shot down by the Fortresses' defensive fire, both pilots being killed. The Focke-Wulfs failed to score but suffered no losses.

Hauptmann Eduard Tratt, the highest-scoring Zerstörer ace of the war. (Author's Collection)

Meanwhile, over northwestern Germany, two FGs totaling 67 Lightnings approached their rendezvous points. Slated to escort Hodges' Liberators to Gotha and LeMay's Fortresses to Schweinfurt, they were recalled just east of Münster, turning west at 1340hrs, leaving the "target area support" to the 57 Mustangs of the 354th and 357th FGs. Crossing the Dutch coast at 1302hrs, it was some time before the P-51s could join the bombers.

Meanwhile, Ibel had launched his main force of interceptors, beginning by scrambling eight Me 110Gs (III./ZG 26) from Wunstorf, followed by Hauptmann Detlev Rohwer's Me 109Gs (II./JG 3) from Rotenburg at 1245hrs, with vectors to form their Gefechtsverband over Kassel. Within the next ten minutes, he reinforced these with II. and III./JG 11 from Wunstorf. From Lützow's 1. Jagddivision, these were augmented by III./JG 54 and I. and II./ZG 26 with orders to assemble over Magdeburg.

The 1st CBW's leading combat wings, headed from Bielefeld to Oscherleben, took the brunt of the defenders' fierce frontal attacks. From 1335–1350hrs, in the vicinity of Bielefeld,

Colonel Claude Putnam's 91st BG lost three Fortresses in quick succession. These were followed by four from Lieutenant Colonel Conway Hall's 381st BG as the dwindling combat wing approached their target.

Finding Oschersleben completely obscured by clouds, the ragged formation turned around and lost three more Fortresses en route to bomb a railways marshaling yard at Bünde, near Minden – one to heavy flak (5./schwere Flak-Abt 321) at 1415hrs while passing Bielefeld, another approaching the new target at 1430hrs, and the third crash-landing near Dortmund at 1440hrs after being badly damaged by fighter attacks.

As the 1st CBW was being slaughtered, Lieutenant Colonel George Bickell's 354th FG showed up with 46 P-51Bs to shepherd Turner's 40th CBW (305th, 306th, and 351st BGs) to Bernburg and, later, Colonel Henry Spicer's 357th FG arrived to escort Travis' 41st CBW formations attacking Halberstadt (379th BG) and Aschersleben (303rd and 384th BGs).

Five minutes after joining the 40th CBW, Captain Robert J. Brooks' 356th FS sighted an estimated 16 Me 110Gs (ZG 26) approaching from 11 o'clock at 23,000ft, escorted by a high cover squadron of Me 109Gs. The two formations clashed and a swirling dogfight began, spiraling downwards. All eight of Major Johann Kogler's III./ZG 26 Zerstörers were lost, along with two from I. Gruppe, four aircrewmen being killed and five wounded. The Me 109G units lost four fighters but no pilots. South of the main battle, Captain Jack T. Bradley's 353rd FS chased the fleeing Zerstörers, eventually shooting down 35-victory ace and II. Gruppe Kommandeur Hauptmann Eduard Tratt in his Me 410A. One P-51B was shot down by an Me 110G, killing the pilot.

Shortly before 1400hrs, as Colonel Maurice "Mo" Preston's 379th BG began their bomb run on Halberstadt, Spicer showed up with 11 Mustangs (of 12 dispatched, one having been shot down by flak over Holland during ingress, the pilot becoming a POW). Accelerating to the front of the bomber formation, Spicer's small group engaged six Me 109Gs preparing to deliver a typical head-on attack, breaking it up.

Clouds obscured the part of Halberstadt containing the Ju 88 component factory, but 18 B-17s dropped their bombloads anyway, the 379th BG's other 19 bombers dropping 110 tons of bombs on the nearby storybook village of Wernigerode. Meanwhile, the 303rd and 384th BGs continued on to Aschersleben, where 34 bombers made an accurate attack. At Bernburg – the deepest penetration of the day – Turner's 40th CBW's 47 B-17s made "a good [bomb] run and created considerable destruction among the installations."

Part of the 40th CBW, Colonel George Robinson's 306th BG, had suffered no losses during the flight to the target, but during the 200-mile return trip to the Dutch coast, their 30 B-17s were now the "tail end Charlie" of the bomber stream and, without escorts, suffered heavily. Launched from Rotenburg at 1424hrs, Major Rolf-Günther Hermichen's I./JG 11 gave chase, caught Robinson's formation south-southwest of Siegen at 1500hrs and, without opposition, shot down five B-17Gs in the next half-hour.

The returning 1st Bomb Division formations were in such disarray that initially the arriving Thunderbolts found no bombers to escort. Colonel Glenn Duncan's 353rd FG arrived over Bonn to find empty skies, but to the northeast, Duncan noticed an airfield – Bonn-Hangelar – stocked with an estimated 40 aircraft. Four flights dived down for a

A 381st BG combat wing formation high above an expansive undercast of clouds over Germany. The nearest aircraft is B-17G S/N 42-31443, unluckily nicknamed "Friday the 13th." It was one of six bombers shot down as the formation approached Oschersleben. (NMUSAF)

strafing pass, and Major Walter Beckham (CO 351st FS) – the Eighth AF's leading ace with 18 victories to his credit – was shot down by flak.

During their low-altitude return flight across Belgium, Duncan shot down a lone Fw 190 for his tenth victory, and one of his flight leaders destroyed a Ju 88 that had apparently just taken off from Diest-Schaffen airfield. Continuing their low-level egress, at 1558hrs, as they crossed the Dutch coast, two 351st FS Thunderbolts were shot down by German flak (3./Flak-Abt 831), both pilots surviving to be captured.

Hoping to intercept the returning bombers on their way home, from 1430–1500hrs Grabmann launched a maximum effort with the II. and III./JG 1, III./JG 2, and I./JG 3. These units intercepted Travis' returning 41st CBW, shooting down two 379th BG Fortresses, one being credited to Heinz Bär (6./JG 1), his second claim of the day.

Led by Major Jack Oberhansly (deputy group CO), the 78th FG arrived over Köln to find the Fortresses under attack by an estimated 30–40 Me 109Gs and Fw 190As, and immediately engaged. The German fighters scattered, most attempting to dive away, but the Thunderbolts quickly overhauled many of them. Six Messerschmitts (III./JG 1 and I./JG 3) and four Focke-Wulfs (III./JG 2) were lost, four pilots being killed. Oberhansly claimed three of these, making him an ace with six "kills".

From 1450–1500hrs, Grabmann also launched I. and II./JG 26. Fw 190As from both groups had recovered to Venlo following their first sortie, where they joined II./JG 2 and IV./ JG 3, forming an ad hoc Jagdgruppe of 30–40 fighters. Taking off, Glunz's 5./JG 26 engaged the returning 41st CBW near Geilenkirchen from 1530–1540hrs, but were warded off by Oberhansly's Thunderbolts, despite several fallacious victory claims.

A little to the northeast, Hauptmann Horst Sternberg (Staka 6./JG 26) led his two wingmen in attacking a crippled, flak-damaged 303rd BG B-17G that was spiraling downwards, trailing thick black smoke. By this time, Lieutenant Colonel Donald Blakeslee's

Death of the Zerstörer King, February 22

Credited with 35 confirmed victories, 24-year old Hauptmann Eduard Tratt was the highest scoring Zerstörer pilot in World War II – his death signaled the end of the Luftwaffe's ability to use the heavily armed twin-engine Me 110G and Me 410s effectively against the increasing American bombing operations against Germany.

Beginning in 1939, Tratt flew the Me 110 heavy fighter with I./ZG 1 during the invasions of Poland and France and was credited with shooting down three Hawker Hurricane fighters over Dunkirk on June 1, 1940. During the next ten weeks of Channel battles, he downed another ten RAF aircraft before being wounded on August 12.

With the Zerstörer's failure as an escort fighter in the Battle of Britain, it was re-roled principally as a ground-attack fighter-bomber and Tratt flew it with great success in the invasion of Russia, during which he was credited with shooting down nine Soviet aircraft and destroying another 17 on the ground, along with 24 tanks and 312 vehicles. He was awarded the *Ritterkreuz des Eisernen Kreuzes* (Knight's Cross of the Iron Cross) on April 12, 1942.

After recovering from wounds a fourth time, he commanded Erprobungskommando 25, testing the new Me 410A-2 Hornisse (*Hornet*) in the heavy bomber interceptor role and shooting down two B-17s in May/June 1943. Consequently, he was given command of the newly resurrected II./ZG 26, flying the Me 410 from Hildesheim in central Germany.

More than eager to take on the USAAF's equivalent heavy fighter – the P-38 – he was also credited with shooting down four Lightnings. His final victory was claimed against one of the retiring 1st Bomb Division Fortresses during the first day of "Big Week."

On February 22, Tratt and his gunner Oberfeldwebel Gillert were reported to have "single-handedly attacked B-17s of the 91st BG" attempting to bomb Oschersleben and their Me 410B-1/U2 may have been damaged by return fire from a 401st BS Fortress. The main attack, however, was to the south where 99 B-17s were bombing Aschersleben, Bernburg, and Halberstadt. These were escorted by 46 P-51s from the 354th FG. During the ensuing battle between the Mustangs and Zerstörers, Captain Jack T. Bradley (CO 353rd FS) and his wingman, Lieutenant Wah Kau Kong, shot down Tratt's Me 410B over the Harz Mountains north of Nordhausen, killing him and his gunner. Immediately afterwards, Kong's P-51B was hit hard by cannon fire from an Me 110G and exploded in mid-air.

351st FS commander Major Walter C. Beckham with his P-47D Little Demon II (S/N 42-75226) shortly after his 18th – and final – aerial victory. Shot down by flak on February 22, 1944, while strafing Bonn-Hangelar airfield, he remained a POW for the duration of the war in Europe. (NARA Ref 3A11484-3A12647)

During his low-level RTB, Lieutenant Colonel Glenn Duncan, 353rd FG CO, "saw a single engine aircraft coming across in front of me at about 500 feet and passing from right to left. I let him pass then fell in behind him and closed to about 50–75 yards. I was so close that I just squeezed the trigger without sighting. He lit up slowly as he slid off on his left wing and crashed near a small town." (NARA)

4th FG had also joined the withdrawing bombers. Sternberg's attack was seen by Major George Carpenter, who led the 335th FS in a diving attack, shooting down Sternberg and one wingman, killing both, while the 78th FG's 83rd FS shot down the third, the pilot bailing out safely. The Fortress crashed just south of Mönchen-Gladbach at 1545hrs; half the crew perished, the rest being captured.

Scrambling from Florennes in Belgium, 7./JG 26's six Fw 190As climbed rapidly with vectors to intercept the next relay of P-47 formations approaching the Saint Trond area. In the last dogfight of the day, the 362nd FG lost one Thunderbolt shot down northeast of Brussels at 1545hrs, killing the pilot. The withdrawing bombers lost one 303rd BG B-17F that crashed 10 miles southeast of Antwerp at 1605hrs and a 306th BG B-17G which crashed southwest of Saint Trond at 1609hrs. In these battles, the ad hoc Jagdgruppe lost six JG 26 Fw 190As and one Me 109G from II./JG 2 shot down, with three pilots killed.

It was another disappointing day for the Eighth AF. Once again adverse weather permitted the bombing of only two of the planned targets. The Junkers Ju 188 assembly plant at Bernburg was heavily damaged; adding to that suffered two days prior, it was now estimated as 70 percent destroyed. The fuselage factory at Aschersleben was considered 50 percent damaged, cutting Ju 88/188 production in half for the next two months. But Williams' 1st Bombardment Division had paid dearly for these modest results.

Schmid's changed tactics – meeting the incoming bombers early and in strength – coupled with the large gaps in the fighter escort coverage, allowed RLV interceptors to exact a high price in bomber losses. I. Jagdkorps had launched 332 sorties, augmented by about one-third of the 406 sorties flown by Luftflotte 3 and 7. Jagddivision, the latter engaging the Fifteenth AF raid on Regensburg. The weather-aborts by two-thirds of the UK-based strike force permitted Schmid's interceptors to concentrate their attacks on the 255 Fortresses over northern Germany. In the battles that ranged across Holland, Germany, and Belgium, the 1st Bombardment Division's main strike force had lost 27 Fortresses.

Additionally, in a rare instance of flak batteries also proving notably successful, five B-17Gs were shot down. Finally, three more Fortresses were ditched or crashed into the North Sea, while, unable to land, a fourth was abandoned over Norfolk and also crashed into the sea. The total of 36 B-17s lost represented 14 percent of the main strike force.

Schmid reported, "Since weather conditions were favorable and high-altitude visibility good, our assembly maneuvers were carried out smoothly and without interference from the enemy … Our fighter aircraft, approaching from the north, were able to make repeated attacks on the bombers and succeeded in bringing down a good number while keeping their own losses to a reasonable minimum."

Where escorts did engage, RLV losses were hardly "a reasonable minimum." While the Luftwaffe Quartermaster recorded the loss of 42 aircraft written off the inventory of Luftflotte Reich and Luftflotte 3, Caldwell's research shows that the actual losses totaled 40 single-engine (21 Me 109G/T and 19 Fw 190As) fighters. Once again the Zerstörers suffered severely; ten Me 110Gs (of 16 launched) and Tratt's Me 410 were lost. Additionally, a dozen single-engine fighter pilots and a like number of Zerstörer aircrewmen were killed in action.

Only three Thunderbolts and a P-51 were lost in air-to-air combat with RLV interceptors, plus another four P-47s and a Mustang were lost to flak. The lopsided battle of attrition continued, with the American fighter pilots dominating the results.

Fifteenth AF Missions, February 22, 23, and 24

The soft underbelly of Fortress Europe did not have the extensive radar network and the sophisticated command and control system enjoyed by the RLV. Consequently, the 204 heavy bombers making up Twining's first full participation in Operation *Argument* had flown halfway to their targets before Jagdfliegerführer Ostmark (or JaFü Ostmark, Fighter Command Austria, 7. Jagddivision's southern sector command) was informed of their approach.

In the air, on the ground: February 22

In his "New Year's Message," USAAF commanding general Henry "Hap" Arnold ordered Eighth AF to "Destroy the Enemy Air Force wherever you find them, in the air, on the ground and in the factories." During "Big Week" VIII Bomber Command was certainly doing its part by destroying German aircraft factories, and VIII Fighter Command was tallying impressive "kill" scores, shooting down Luftwaffe interceptors attempting to get at the bombers. In addition, the fighter groups – especially the P-47 Thunderbolt-equipped units – took the war to the enemy by "beating them up on the ground on the way home."

To encourage airfield strafing attacks, Eighth AF soon announced that an aircraft destroyed on the ground would count equally with those downed in air-to-air combat. The command's first successful airfield strafing mission was conducted by 356th FG on January 21, 1944, with two enemy aircraft claimed destroyed and two more damaged.

But it was Colonel Glenn Duncan (CO 353rd FG) who pioneered Eighth AF's airfield strafing tactics. On the third day of "Big Week," after arriving over Bonn to cover the B-17s' withdrawal, Duncan's 353rd FG found no enemy interceptors present, but looking northeast, he saw an estimated 40 aircraft on the ground at Hangelar airfield (home of I./JG 300). Detailing Major Walter Beckham (CO 351st FS) – the Eighth AF's leading ace with 18 victories to his credit – to provide high cover, Duncan dived down with eight P-47Ds to strafe a row of Ju 88s. Pulling up after his firing pass, he circled his two flights around the field to ward off any enemy fighters and called Beckham down to continue the attack.

Accelerating to 425mph in his dive, Beckham led his flight of four across the airfield at very low level, lining up to strafe a row of six aircraft, while Captain Gordon Compton aimed his flight at three others. Compton later described, "As I closed I saw three Fw 190s parked close together. I strafed and saw hits on all three, and saw one burst into flames. I pulled up off the target, turning about 90 degrees to the left and heard Major Beckham say that he'd been hit, was on fire and for everyone to get out. I was about 500 feet high at this time and saw tracers coming from every direction, also flak was bursting uncomfortably close, so I hit the deck."

Beckham had indeed been hit (by lichte Flak-Abteilung 784's single 8.8cm battery), an 88mm shell bursting beneath the nose of his P-47D-11 "Little Demon II" (42-75226 YJ-Y) and crippling its big radial engine, setting it ablaze. Immediately he called to his wingman, Lieutenant George Perpente, "Stay down, take the boys home, George. I can't make it." Beckham pulled up, rolled over and bailed out and was soon captured, remaining a POW for the rest of the war. It was a fate that would befall several notable Eighth AF aces in future airfield attacks as the American fighters soon roamed all across Germany.

Compton was credited with one Fw 190 destroyed and two damaged in this attack.

GRAHAM TURNER

Taking off from Italian airfields around Foggia, Manduria, and Cerignola, 86 B-17s and 118 B-24s flew up the Adriatic Sea, splitting the distance between Luftwaffe forces in Italy (Luftflotte 2) and Yugoslavia (Luftwaffekommando Süd-Ost, Luftwaffe Command, South-East), bound for Regensburg in southeast Germany. The target for Brigadier General Charles Lawrence's 5th BW was the Me 109G component factory in the city's western suburb of Prüfening, while Liberators from Brigadier General Joseph Atkinson's 47th BW were to strike the large assembly plant at Obertraubling, south of the city. As a diversion, in Yugoslavia, 28 B-17s attacked Zagreb airfield and the newly formed 304th BW's Liberators went on a practice mission to attack the harbor at Sibenek.

The planned times over targets for the main strike force were coordinated so that the Italy-based bombers were to arrive over Regensburg just as LeMay's 333 Fortresses were bombing Schweinfurt, thus splitting Huth's defences between two large – and hopefully overwhelming – strike forces.

Each of Twining's two formations was to be supported a group of P-38s (14th and 82nd FGs) in the target area and escorted out, but their timing was off and they were never in position to engage the responding Luftwaffe interceptors. With 63 P-47Ds, the 325th FG was scheduled to provide withdrawal support over the Adriatic.

From 1142–1145hrs – as the leading bomber formations began crossing Italy's Tyrolean Alps 150–200 miles from their targets – Oberst Gotthard Handrick (JaFü Ostmark) launched Major Gerhard Michalski's II./JG 53 (Me 109Gs) from Vienna-Seyring and Hauptmann Egon Albrecht's II./ZG 1 (Me 110Gs) from Wels. These were followed 15 minutes later by Hauptmann Ludwig "Ziskus" Franzisket's I./JG 27 (Me 109Gs) – reinforced with eight more Gustavs flown by instructors and students of the co-located *Verbändeführer Schule* (formation leaders school), scrambling from Fels-am-Wagram, just west of Vienna. This formation was ordered to assemble its Gefechtsverband over Vienna and then fly to Linz, where the controller issued vectors towards the American bombers. Launched late from as far away as 180 miles east of the bombers' northerly route, the Austrian-based fighters found themselves in a long tail chase and only intercepted the two formations following their bomb runs over their two targets.

Without needing to defend against the Eighth AF's planned strike against Schweinfurt, Huth's 7. Jagddivision was able to meet the threat approaching from the south with full force and, around noon, launched two Jagdgruppen (I./JG 5 and II./JG 27), one Zerstörergruppe (II./ZG 76), one Wild Sau Gruppe (I./JG 301) and a fighter training unit (I./JG 104). Altogether, about 200 interceptors were launched.

From Neubiberg, Major Walter Brede's I./JG 301 Wild Sau Me 109G-6s intercepted the approaching enemy over the Austrian Alps about 125 miles from their targets, but were once again unsuccessful at bringing down any American bombers. Two of Brede's night-interceptors were shot down, both pilots bailing out safely.

Temporarily based at Obertraubling airfield to re-equip with new BR 21-armed Me 109G-6s, Major Erich Gerlitz's I./JG 5 intercepted next and claimed to have shot down three Flying Fortresses without loss. These were soon joined by Major Werner Schroer's II./JG 27, launching from Wiesbaden-Erbenheim, who claimed one Fortress shot down (and a P-47) for the loss of two Gustavs with one pilot wounded.

The effect was far greater than the actual result. As 301st BG bombardier John T. Upton later reported, "Once past the Alps, the fighters then moved upon our lead formation so we speeded up and formed in with the 97th [Bombardment Group] for protection. We got some trouble there but it looked and felt good to be among a Group we knew and trusted and fought back like demons. The formation was so tight that it seemed that anyone

Major General Nathan F. Twining, commander of USAAF Fifteenth Air Force. (USAF Photo)

could walk from one plane wingtip to another – or the waist gunner could jump out of his opening and land on the wing of the plane next to him."

Of the 86 B-17s approaching Regensburg, only 65 from the 97th and 301st BGs found the Prüfening component factory, dropping 153 tons of bombs at 1230hrs, then turned left to head south for Munich. One group (21 B-17s) failed to locate the target and dumped 42 tons of bombs on the Peterhausen railway marshaling yards, just north of Munich, at 1258hrs.

Once Lawrence's 5th BW was headed south again, 4. Staffel of Michalski's II./JG 53 finally intercepted the Flying Fortresses, 32-victory *experte* Oberfeldwebel Stefan "Steff" Litjen claiming the shooting down of three bombers, but losing one of his squadron mates to their defensive fire, the pilot being killed.

Also attacking the egressing Fortresses was Major Herbert Kaminski's II./ZG 76, which lost two Me 110Gs – all four crewmen killed – without claiming a single victory. Much better luck was had by Oberleutnant Fritz Stehle's 5./ZG 26, who launched from Oberpfaffenhofen (near Munich) on a practice mission with ten BK 5-armed Me 410A-1/U4s. Despite not yet being operational with the large 5cm cannon, north of

Generalleutnant Joachim-Friedrich Huth, commander of 7. Jagddivision. (Author's Collection)

Munich the Staffel claimed to have shot down two 97th BG B-17s, the second one falling to Stehle just south of Dachau. Lawrence's 5th BW actually lost a total of five B-17s on this mission.

Meanwhile, Atkinson's 47th BW struck Obertraubling "with good effect" but lost two bombers (376th BG) that collided over the target after being damaged by flak. The Liberators turned to the northeast to reform after their bomb runs, and beginning at 1248hrs were intercepted by Albrecht's II./ZG 1 southeast of Pilsen as they turned south for their flight back to Italy. The Zerstörers claimed eight B-24s shot down – one of them by Albrecht – but lost four Me 110Gs to the Liberators' defensive fire, with one pilot killed and another wounded.

Along with Albrecht's Zerstörers, Franzisket's Gustavs intercepted Atkinson's B-24s, claiming to shoot down another four bombers. The I./JG 27 lost three Me 109Gs to the Liberators' defensive fire, with two pilots killed and the third wounded. Joining the south-bound running battle near Straubing, at 1320hrs Oberfeldwebel Herbert Rollage (5./JG 53) heavily damaged one bomber and claimed it as a Herausschuss for his 50th confirmed victory. Atkinson's 47th BW lost a total of 14 Liberators, a heavy attrition of 12 percent of the strike

B-17F-95-BO, S/N 42-30267 "Hustlin' Huzzy" (97th BG, 341st BS) crossing the Alps. (USAF Photo)

force, but caused significant damage to the Me 109G assembly plant at Obertraubling. The Messerschmitt component factory at Prüfening was not so badly hit and would have to be struck again. Of the estimated 120 interceptors engaging the Fifteenth AF formations, Huth's 7. Jagddivision lost 15 aircraft, including eight Me 109Gs and six Me 110Gs, with eight pilots being killed in the battle.

The next day, the Eighth AF stood down – ostensibly because the high pressure area over Bavaria had dissipated and all planned targets would be obscured by clouds. But it was more than that: after three days at full cry, launching 2,663 sorties with their 1,304 serviceable heavy bombers, the command needed a break before continuing at Anderson's grueling maximum effort pace. The 94 bombers lost were easily replaced, typically a process that

took two days. But of the 1,210 remaining, 486 had suffered battle damage, some of them more than once. While most of the repairs were simple sheet metal patches over bullet holes, many were more extensive and time-consuming, such as engine replacements or structural repairs. The attrition effects of reduced serviceability due to battle damage are seen in the steady decline in the number of bombers dispatched during the first three days of *Argument* – 1,003, 861, and 799 – while of the 754 bombers returning from the third day's missions, 146 were damaged, many needing significant repairs. The command's mechanics and engineers needed a day to fix as many as possible before another maximum effort could be mounted.

Likewise, almost all of the 1,310 aircrews had flown at least two of the three missions and were spent, needing a rest – a day without the bone-wearying tension of flying in winter weather and the emotional and psychological trauma of relentless combat. Flying on instruments or in close formation in such weather is both a muscle-tensing and nerve-rackingly intense physical exercise, and to do so for hours on end for several days in a row is chronically fatiguing, frequently leading to misjudgments, mid-air collisions, and crashes. Coupled with this, the acutely unnerving stress of going into – and surviving – one deadly encounter after another can completely drain a combat aviator. Consequently, in order to continue, a day to regroup was desperately needed before resuming the Eighth AF's participation in the campaign.

From Italy, Fifteenth AF was in much better shape to continue the pressure on Luftflotte Reich, and planned a major mission to Steyr in Austria to attack the Walzlagerwerke ball-bearing manufacturer and the Steyr-Daimler-Puch aircraft component factory. Twining dispatched 166 bombers, but Lawrence's 57 B-17s (5th BW) aborted due to weather, leaving 109 B-24s from Atkinson's 47th BW to bomb the Walzlagerwerke plant. This facility previously produced 10 percent of Germany's anti-friction bearings, but was in the process of increasing production by 50 percent to make up for losses experienced at Schweinfurt.

Continuing "snafus" plagued Lieutenant Colonel Paul Blanchard's 306th Fighter Wing, leaving Atkinson's raiders unprotected during their approach to Steyr. Of the 89 Lightnings flying effective missions, Lieutenant Colonel Oliver Taylor's P-38Js (14th FG), scheduled for target area support, arrived late – after the Liberators had completed their bomb runs – and Lieutenant Colonel Robert Richard's P-38Hs (1st FG) provided withdrawal support.

From 1108–1113hrs – as the leading bomber formations crossed the Adriatic coast near Trieste about 180 miles from their targets – Handrick launched Franzisket's and Michalski's

A Schwarm of 6./ZG 26 Bf 110G-2s fly in typical winter weather over snow-covered terrain of southern Germany in February, 1944. (Bundesarchiv, Bild 101I-663-6737-19, Fotograf(in): Hebenstreit)

Gustavs (I./JG 27 and II./JG 53) and Albrecht's Zerstörers (II./ZG 1). Once again without the need to defend against the UK-based Eighth AF, at 1115hrs Huth's 7. Jagddivision began launching a full response to meet the approaching Fifteenth AF formations, scrambling two Jagdgruppen (III./JG 3 and II./JG 27), two Zerstörergruppe (I. and II./ZG 76), and one Nachtjagdgruppe (II./NJG 6). Altogether, 197 interceptors were launched.

Atkinson's strike force approached in two combat wings, the second (98th and 376th BGs) following seven minutes behind the first (449th, 450th, and 451st BGs). Arrowing towards their target, located midway between Vienna and Wels, the leading formation became the focal point of Handrick's interceptors, with Albrecht's Zerstörers beginning the battle with BR 21 rockets – firing salvoes of two from 1,000 yards astern – as the bombers passed Klagenfurt, then closed and attacked with cannon and machine guns.

Lieutenant Ben Konsynski, a 376th BG pilot leading the group's nine-plane C Section (the group's low combat squadron), reported:

> About 20 minutes from the target our formation was attacked by 75 to 100 German aircraft, there were Bf 109s, Bf 110s, and Fw 190s [sic]. We lacked air cover at this point. When we saw the enemy planes attacking the high boxes, it took a few minutes to tighten up our section and move in close to 'A' and 'B' sections of our formation. When I next looked up I saw three B-24s coming down out of control from 'B' Section. The Germans were shooting rockets and 20mm cannon with telling effect. The attack continued from that point up to target. In the low section we were not getting the brunt of the attack until inexplicably the formation leader of the lead group [98th BG] decided to turn off course, without notice, and head back. We had not reached the IP [initial point] so we continued on alone and that is when we were hit by rocket and cannon fire from attacking planes.

Albrecht's Zerstörers shot down four Liberators. Engaging the lead combat wing at noon about 25 miles south of Steyr, Franzisket's Me 109Gs brought down three more prior to the target, but the ferocity of their attacks shattered the leading formation. From the trailing 376th BG, one aircrewman reported:

> Bombers that preceded us to the target were returning and they approached us head on at lower altitudes. Their condition was noticeably critical. Formations were almost non-existent and many planes were on fire.
>
> As we approached the target, the German fighters, mainly Bf 109s, began attacking [our] formations. The entire formation in front and to the right of us disappeared [this was the 98th BG turning away] within a short time and it was then that we were attacked… I watched them as they hit the eleven planes in the high [squadron] formation. They were attacking with about seven to ten fighters in succession and in their first pass downed 'Tail-end Charlie.' In about ten minutes they wiped out the high element, attacking from every hour of the clock. Then they hit our element and we fought them into the target. That battle into the target probably lasted 30 minutes.

A 450th BG pathfinder B-24 Liberator (S/N 41-28774) over the Alps. (USAF)

With the 98th BG shearing away prior to the IP, between 1208 and 1215hrs just 81 B-24s bombed the target, but only the 21 Liberators of the 376th BG actually hit the Walzlagerwerke factory, their 52 tons of bombs still causing severe damage to the 100,000sqft facility.

Engaging the second combat wing were Major Walther Dahl's two dozen Gustavs (III./JG 3). Together with Franzisket's Jagdgruppe, they shot down another ten bombers before Taylor's Lightnings (14th FG) arrived to rescue them. The P-38Js quickly destroyed two Me 110Gs, killing all four crewmen, and chased away the Me 109Gs, thus ending the massacre.

For the loss of nine Me 109Gs to the bombers' defensive fire – with three pilots being killed – I./JG 27 pilots claimed to have shot down 14 B-24s in 20 minutes of combat, and III./JG 3 pilots put in claims for downing 15 bombers and seven Lightnings. Of the 29 bombers claimed, only 13 victories were confirmed by OKL administrators. Dahl had a reputation for over claiming, allowing many of his pilots' claims to be filed without crash witnesses, thus inflating his group's statistics for the OKW's evening press release. However, these unverified victories were almost never confirmed by the OKL. Dahl himself was credited with one Liberator and a Lightning, bringing his total score to 61, but no P-38s were lost on this mission.

Even with the severe over claiming by the Jadgwaffe pilots, the high losses (15 percent of the attacking force) and the psychological shock of the Messerschmitts' fierce attacks resulted in this raid being remembered as "the Fifteenth AF's Schweinfurt." As one 376th BG tail-gunner stated, "never before or since did I see the enemy so wildly aggressive, pressing their attacks in very close." In the final analysis, all that could be said was it would have been much worse if the other two Jagdgruppen (II./JG 27 and II./JG 53) and Oberstleutnant Robert Kowalewski's Zerstörers (ZG 76) had also managed to intercept Atkinson's bombers.

Having knocked out 20 percent of Walzlagerwerke's ball-bearing production, Twining sent Lawrence's 5th BW back to Steyr the following day to hit the Daimler-Puch factory, a "do over" for the mission aborted the day before. Lawrence launched a maximum effort: 140 B-17s – making up two combat wings – from all four bomb groups. Of these, 26 aborted for various mechanical reasons, while the 99th BG became separated from the rest of the strike force and its 27 Fortresses bombed the secondary target – the Ramsa oil refinery and Silurificio Whitehead torpedo factory at Fiume (now Rijeka, Croatia) – losing one bomber to flak over the targets.

Major Walther Dahl, commander of III./JG 3. (Author's Collection)

The remaining 87 B-17s – led by Colonel Frank Allen's 97th BG – were to be escorted out of the target area by an equal number of Lightnings (1st and 82nd FGs) and 59 Thunderbolts (325th FG). However, Lieutenant Colonel Robert Baseler's P-47Ds were operating at the very limits of their effective range and had no fuel for combat, so they played no part in the battle over Steyr. To maximize the fighter coverage, Allen's formations flew a direct route to the target, providing plenty of warning to Handrick and his Jafü Ostmark controllers.

At 1130hrs, Handrick scrambled Albrecht's Zerstörers from Wels, then 30 minutes later (1154–1200hrs) launched his two Jagdgruppen (I./JG 27 and II./JG 53) from their bases near Vienna and Linz. Twining hoped that the Eighth AF's near simultaneous mission to Schweinfurt would draw off Huth's 7. Jagddivision interceptors, but this would not be the case. Huth's command launched two Jagdgruppen (III./JG 3 and II./JG 27), one Wild Sau Staffel (1./JG 301), two Zerstörergruppen (ZG 76, which had forward-deployed south to Wels that morning), and three night-fighter training units (II./NJG 101 and I. and II./NJG 102). Altogether, 243 interceptors sortied to meet Twining's raiders.

Handrick's controllers quickly recognized that Allen's bombers were headed directly to Steyr, and vectored all responding units to intercept. Albrecht's Zerstörers engaged the approaching Fortresses 100 miles south of the target, initiating an hour-long running battle.

About 20 Me 110Gs intercepted, firing rockets from long range before closing for cannon attacks, claiming one bomber shot down before the first of approximately 110 Me 109Gs arrived.

These were Franzisket's I./JG 27, reinforced again by a few Gustavs of the Verbändeführer Schule, followed by Michalski's II./JG 53. Free from any interference by escort fighters, the Me 109G pilots made a single head-on pass through Allen's leading formation to concentrate their attacks on the 33 B-17s (of 37 dispatched) of the 2nd BG. Now the sole component of the trailing formation, Colonel Herbert Rice's group was aggressively assaulted from astern – from positions at 4 to 8 o'clock – by four-ship Schwäme formations that pressed their attacks to within 150ft. Ten B-17s fell prior to reaching the target and the formation was broken up by the fierce attacks. One of these fell to Michalski as his 62nd victory. However, driving their attacks deep into the Fortresses' vicious defensive fire, eight Me 109Gs were lost, with one pilot killed and six more wounded.

The two dozen Gustavs of Dahl's III./JG 3 – reinforced by 1./JG 301 – intercepted Allen's leading combat wing as they began releasing their bombloads on the target. Attacking just as fiercely, they quickly shot down three 301st BG Fortresses but lost four fighters, with one pilot killed. Despite the savage attacks, between 1306 and 1310hrs, Allen's formations unleashed 261 tons of bombs on the target, "virtually obliterating the aircraft component plant. Two bombs even found their way into the nearby ball-bearing factory and destroyed two months' worth of semi-finished production."

Turning south for the return flight to Foggia, Allen's strike force offered their "six o'clock" to Kowalewski's Stab and II./ZG 76, as well as the night-fighter training units joining the battle from the north. The Zerstörers focused their attacks on Rice's shattered formation, concentrating on the stragglers, helping the engaged fighters shoot down three more 2nd BG Fortresses. As the first Lightnings arrived, Allen sent them to the rear to rescue the group's 20 surviving Fortresses.

The P-38s shot down two ZG 76 Me 110s and three Do 217Ns from II./NJG 101 and II./NJG 102, but lost one to a II./ZG 1 Zerstörer. Fourteen Lightnings from Richard's 71st FS – led by Group Operations Officer Lieutenant Colonel Burton McKenzie – engaged Dahl's III./JG 3 and claimed two Me 109Gs, but McKenzie was shot down and killed. Dahl claimed one P-38, along with two B-17s, shot down in this battle.

Altogether, Lawrence's 5th BW lost 17 B-17s on the mission, with another written off as salvage upon return. Of these, 16 were lost from the 87 that pressed on to Steyr, a loss rate of 18 percent. Once again, it would have been even worse if the other 100 interceptors launched had been able to engage Allen's formations.

Of the approximately 142 interceptors attacking the raiders, Huth's 7. Jagddivision, including his southern JaFü Ostmark, lost 12 Me 109Gs, two Zerstörers, and three night-fighters, with four aircrewmen killed and eight wounded. This was a very low price to pay for such decimating attrition inflicted upon Twining's bomber forces.

Eighth AF Mission No.233, February 24

As Twining's 77 B-17s were pummeling the Steyr-Daimler-Puch Me 109G component factory, Doolittle's 505 raiders were within 12–30 minutes of releasing over 1,000 tons of high explosives and incendiaries on their targets: the Gothaer Waggonfabrik (GWF) Me 110 final assembly plant and Schweinfurt's four Vereinigte Kugellager Fabriken (VKF) AG factories, which were still working at 73 percent capacity despite previous damage and Speer's ongoing industry dispersal program. The clear weather permitted Williams' 1st Bombardment Division to strike the latter – to make up for LeMay's weather-aborted mission two days before – and Hodges' Liberators to attempt completing the destruction of the Luftwaffe's largest Me 110/410 production facility by adding to the damage done by Colonel Jack Wood's 20th CBW on the opening day of the offensive.

Fifteenth Air Force's Contribution to "Big Week": 22 February 1944

The Fifteenth AF's first target was the Messerschmitt manufacturing complex at Regensburg however the raid was aborted due to adverse weather. Two days later 204 heavy bombers struck the Me 109G production facility, but 17 were lost to Luftwaffe interceptors. The Obertraubling assembly plant was seriously damaged; the Prüfening component factory less so, and was re-attacked during "Big Week."

Pilsen

Schweinfurt

GERMANY

Regensburg

5

4

C

D

B

A

6

Peterhausen

E

Augsburg

Munich

Innsbruck

Major Eighth AF Units: ●

1. 5th Bombardment Wing (B-17s)
2. 47th Bombardment Wing (B-24s)
3. 325th Fighter Group (P-47s)

EVENTS

1. 1100hrs: Fifteenth AF's 5th and 47th Bomb Wings cross the Italian Adriatic Coast northbound. Navigators aim to cross the Alps' Hohen Tauer mountain range through the "saddle" between Großvenediger (12,028ft) and Großglockner (12,461ft) peaks.

2. 1142hrs: Having monitored the approach of the Fifteenth AF bombers through the radio listening service, JaFü Ostmark begins launching its interceptors, vectoring them east initially, resulting in falling well behind the bombers as they turn towards Regensburg.

3. 1200hrs: 7. Jagddivision launches its first interceptors, I./JG 301 intercepting over the Alps, followed by I./JG 5 and II./JG 27, claiming four B-17s shot down.

4. 1230hrs: 5th Bomb Division (65 B-17s) attack the Prüfening Me 109G component factory. Under attack by 4./JG 53 Me 109Gs, only a few hits are scored. The formation turns left towards Munich to egress the target area. 47th Bomb Wing (116 B-24s) causes significant damage to the Obertraubling Me 109G assembly plant, after which they turn northeast towards Pilsen to egress the target area.

5. 1248hrs: Once reformed, the 47th Bomb Wing turns south to withdraw and is finally intercepted by I./JG 27, 5./JG 53, and I./ZG 1, claiming 12 Liberators shot down, most of them by Me 110Gs. The B-24s return via their ingress routing.

6. 1258hrs: After turning towards Munich one BG attacks a secondary target, the Peterhausen railway yards. The 82 B-17s are intercepted by Me 110Gs (II./ZG 76) and Me 410s (5./ZG 26), losing one bomber to the Me 410s' 5cm cannon attacks.

7. 1435hrs: The last Fifteenth AF bombers are joined by 325th FG (63 P-47s) as they cross the coast headed for their bases in southern Italy. Total bomber losses are five B-17s and 14 B-24s (two to flak). The Luftwaffe lost eight Me 109Gs and six Me 110Gs.

AUSTRIA

G

2 Vienna

F

Wiener Neustadt

Linz

Steyr

CZECH REPUBLIC

KEY

| | Bombers under attack

✈ Airfield

▲ Target

Graz

urg

YUGOSLAVIA

Klagenfurt

Zagreb

Luftwaffe Interceptor Units: ●

7. Jagddivision
A. I./JG 5   Regensburg-Obertraubling
B. II./JG 27   Wiesbaden-Erbenheim
C. I./JG 301 and II./ZG 76   Neubiberg
D. I./ZG 76   Ansbach
E. 5./ZG 26   Oberpfaffenhofen
JaFü Ostmark
F. I./JG 27   Fels-am-Wagram
G. II./JG 53   Vienna-Seyring
H. II./ZG 1   Wels

Udine

Trieste   Fiume

1

7

3   2

Venice   1

ITALY

ADRIATIC SEA

Meanwhile, in a repeat of the first day's operation, LeMay's longer-ranged 3rd Bomb Division would try again against the Tutow and Krzesiny Fw 190 factories and the training center at Kreising airfield near Poznań. Anticipating bad weather across northern and eastern Germany, LeMay's five combat wings were led by the 482nd BG Pathfinders, who would provide radar-directed blind bombing of the Marienehe Heinkel Flugzeugwerke bomber factory near Rostock in the event the primary targets were obscured by cloud.

LeMay's 304 Flying Fortresses took off first, assembled into five combat wings, and once again headed off across the North Sea towards Denmark, permitting Kepner's VIII FC to use its 609 Thunderbolts, 70 Lightnings, and 88 Mustangs to cover Anderson's main strike force of 266 B-17s and 239 B-24s, which would head eastbound for the Dutch coast much as they had on February 20.

Having seen an almost identical pattern develop only four days before, Schmid and Grabmann were not going to be so easily fooled this time. Anticipating another major effort, Schmid requested reinforcement from Luftflotte 3 and received II. and III./JG 2 from Generalmajor Karl Hentschel's 5. Jagddivision, the two Jagdgruppen arriving at Rheine about 1030hrs.

Paving the way for Doolittle's heavy bombers, the brilliant weather – reported as "clear and visibility excellent" – allowed Ninth AF to send 226 Marauders to attack Luftwaffe airfields at Gilze-Rijen, Deelen, and Leeuwarden in a series of group-size raids that lasted an hour (0957–1056hrs). These were the home bases to two night-fighter units – IV./NJG 1's Me 110G-4s and III./NJG 2's Ju 88C-6s – so Grabmann's day-fighter force was not affected.

Midway through the Marauder attacks, LeMay's force, estimated at 200 bombers, was detected at 1016hrs some 75 miles west of Texel island, headed northeast, tracked all the way to Denmark by the Flugmeldedienst's coastal EW radars. Almost an hour later (1109hrs), the Funkaufklärungsdienst reported that an estimated 400 bombers were assembling over England. Soon these would be headed across the Channel, approaching the Dutch coast between Den Helder and Ijmuiden.

Anticipating the approach of the Eighth AF's main force, Grabmann began scrambling his interceptors at 1058hrs and called for reinforcements from Oberst Carl Vieck's 4. Jagddivision, leaving to 2. Jagddivision LeMay's diversion as it angled towards Denmark. Ibel husbanded his larger day-fighter units, intending to intercept the main force as they approached the Dutch–German border, and assigned the diversionary force to Major Müller-Rendsberg's Jagdschnittsführer-Dänemark. The thick, extensive overcast and heavy icing conditions precluded the use of his single-engine, single-seat fighters (10. and 11./JG 11), so Oberst Günther Lützow provided all of his available twin-engine night-fighters (NJG 5), reinforced by others (NJG 6) from Huth's 7. Jagddivision. These Me 110Gs flew north to join Müller-Rendsberg's Ju 88Cs (IV./NJG 3) and intercepted the 3rd Bomb Division over the Bay of Lübeck, just northwest of Rostock.

Approaching Rostock, two 385th BG Fortresses were shot down and one from 388th BG was damaged so badly it had to escape to Sweden. Two more B-17s (95th and 452nd BGs) were lost on the return flight. Although they damaged another 60 bombers and wounded eight crewmen, the night-fighters suffered heavily from the Fortresses' defensive fire – six Me 110Gs and one Ju 88C were lost, with ten crewmen killed.

The assigned targets were covered by a thick continuous blanket of cloud, forcing the attackers to

Paving the way for the Eighth AF's heavy bombers, Ninth AF B-26 Marauders of the 387th Bomb Group devastate Leeuwarden airfield, near the Dutch coast, on February 24, 1944. (NMUSAF)

resort to radar bombing. Two of the Tutow-targeted combat wings successfully released on Rostock's Heinkel works at 1240hrs. The third Pathfinder accidently released prior to the target and the 60 B-17s following him did likewise, their loads falling harmlessly into the sea. The two combat wings heading to Poznań dropped their loads "on an aircraft factory" in the town of Gnesen (now Gniezno, Poland) at 1404hrs. Luftwaffe records reported, "The damage in Rostock and Gnesen was relatively slight."

Meanwhile, with inflight visibility exceeding 50 miles on this crystal-clear day, Brigadier General Edward Timberlake's 2nd CBW led the 14th and 20th CBWs in a long procession of Liberator formations flying across northern Holland at 16,000–21,500ft in order to increase their bombing accuracy. However, at that altitude the winds were much stronger than forecast, and soon the stream of bombers were flying across the IJsselmeer – headed towards Osnabrück – well ahead of their escorts.

Trailing Timberlake's three combat wings came Turner's 40th CBW, leading a column of five B-17 combat wings, flying at the usual altitudes of 22,000–25,000ft, escorted across the sea by 11 RAF squadrons. Taking off from airfields near Lille and Laon in France and the Belgian town of Florennes between 1055 and 1100hrs, JG 26's three Jagdgruppen climbed for altitude and angled northeast to intercept the bomber stream near the Dutch–German border. Hauptmann Karl Borris's I. Gruppe caught Timberlake's 2nd CBW – and made one firing pass, shooting down a single 445th BG B-24H – before they had to land at Rheine, out of fuel from the long chase. Major Wilhelm Gäth's Fw 190As and Major Klaus Mietusch's Me 109Gs arrived before the first relay of Thunderbolts and quickly shot down two 92nd BG and two 306th BG Fortresses, killing 20 crewmen, the other 30 being captured.

Having shot down four of the B-17Gs, Mietusch's III. Gruppe was attacked near Lingen by Colonel Avelin Tacon's 359th FG Thunderbolts. The Gustav pilots attempted to dive away but were quickly overhauled by the faster, heavier P-47Ds and four were shot down, all four pilots being killed. One Thunderbolt was lost, the pilot being killed, shot down by a 12. Staffel pilot (no victory claimed) "while attacking another Me 109."

While Oberst Josef "Pips" Priller's JG 26 was intercepting the American bombers, at 1058hrs Grabmann scrambled Buhligen's II./JG 2 from Rheine, followed half an hour later by his main force – Oberst Walter "Gulle" Oesau's Stab, I., and II./JG 1, reinforced by 25 Fw 190As from III./JG 2 and four more from II./JG 300. These were to be supported by I. and IV./JG 3, launching from Venlo and Volkel in Holland. Oesau's JG 1 units climbed eastwards as they joined into a Gefechtsverband, and once organized, they reversed course to attack Hodges' Liberators while the JG 2 and 3 units attempted individual interceptions.

As the first relay of Thunderbolts turned back for England, Zemke's 56th FG joined the Fortresses over Holland, escorting them as far as Herford, where they were to turn south for Schweinfurt. As they arrived, the leading combat wing reported being under attack and, accelerating to the front of the bomber stream, Zemke attacked a Schwarm of Fw 190As (II./JG 300) while Major James Stewart, leading the 61st FS, engaged Me 109Gs (II./JG 2) that immediately dived away.

In wide-ranging combats, battling the 56th, 78th, and 352nd FGs, JGs 2 and 3 lost nine Me 109Gs, with three pilots killed. Hauptmann Kurd Peters' Wild Sau II./JG 300 lost three of its four Fw 190As, reducing that unit to one serviceable airplane and 12 pilots. The Americans lost no P-47Ds in these engagements.

Oberst Günther Lützow was a supremely successful Luftwaffe fighter pilot, having first claimed five victories in the Spanish Civil War and being credited with 102 victories before being posted to Adolf Galland's General der Jagdflieger staff in August 1942. Having commanded a Jagdstaffel in Spain, and JG 3 in the Battle of Britain and against Russia, in September 1943 he became the commander of 1. Jagddivision. (Author's Collection)

Shown here as a Leutnant commanding 9./JG 52 in January 1942, 207-victory ace Oberstleutnant Hermann Graf commanded JG 11 during Operation *Argument*. He was credited with shooting down a B-24 Liberator on January 24, 1944. (Author's Collection)

When Colonel James Stone's 78th FG rendezvoused with their bombers and found the leading Fortresses under attack, Major Jesse Davis' 83rd FS raced ahead to engage. West of Dümmer Lake, they caught 25 Fw 190s (III./JG 2) preparing to attack the bombers. Engaging immediately, the Thunderbolts quickly shot down four Focke-Wulfs, killing two pilots and wounding the other two, and dispersed the rest. The 78th FG lost no P-47Ds in this combat.

Oesau's JG 1 Gefechtsverband intercepted Timberlake's 2nd CBW as they turned southeast at Osnabrück. Striking first was II. Gruppe, Heinz Bär leading a classic diving attack out of the sun, while Major Rudolf-Emil Schnoor's I. Gruppe made a typical head-on attack, the two Jagdgruppen claiming to shoot down nine B-24s. Only two Liberators – B-24Hs from 445th BG – were actually lost, both crashing near Herford between 1240 and 1245hrs.

These attacks were interrupted by the arrival of Colonel Glenn Duncan's 353rd FG. Duncan reported that no enemy fighters were seen until his Thunderbolts were "called up to the lead boxes," where "I saw about 10–12 Fw 190s coming in on the Libs [B-24s] at 10 o'clock so [we] went down. The Fws were just going up on the B-24s' bellies but were sorta [sic] discouraged when we came in on them." JG 1 lost eight Fw 190As, with four pilots killed and two wounded, while Duncan's unit had no losses.

When Hodges' Liberators made their turn at Osnabrück they were 11 minutes ahead of schedule, leaving a long gap before the "target area support" escorts – 55th FG Lightnings and 357th FG Mustangs – could join them. In the meantime, from 1201–1215hrs, Ibel scrambled his main force: all three Jagdgruppen of Oberstleutnant Hermann Graf's JG 11 plus II./JG 3 from Rotenburg and the pitiful remnant (four Me 110Gs) of Major Johann Kogler's III./ZG 26. To reinforce the latter, Lützow launched ten Me 110Gs from I./ZG 26, plus Oberstleutnant Anton Mader's III./JG 54, a dozen Wild Sau Me 109Gs (I./JG 300) and a few Me 410s (II./ZG 26). The 14 Me 110Gs assembled together at 23,000ft over Brauschweig and were joined by Hauptmann Günther Specht's II./JG 11 as their fighter escort, and at 1215hrs, Kogler led the entire formation southeast, finally catching the bombers in the target area.

Racing ahead of the slower Zerstörers, Graf's Gefechtsverband – minus Hauptmann "Toni" Hackl's III. Gruppe – caught the Liberators at 1305hrs as they approached Eisenach and turned left, realigning their formations for their bomb runs on Gotha. Hauptmann Rolf Hermichen's I./JG 11 attacked immediately, followed quickly by II./JG 3, led by Geschwaderkommodore Oberstleutnant Wolf-Dietrich Wilcke, a 154-victory ace.

Flying at altitudes in the heart of the Fw 190A's optimum operating envelope, Graf's Focke-Wulfs and Wilcke's Me 109Gs caused a massacre. In the space of half an hour – 1305–1335hrs – they shot down ten of Timberlake's 2nd CBW Liberators in the target area and six more from the following 14th CBW. Kogler's Zerstörers soon joined the slaughter, attacking the trailing 20th CBW and using rockets to shoot down three Liberators between 1320 and 1350hrs.

Finally catching up with their charges, the scheduled target area escorts could not stop the massacre. Led by Major Mark Shipman, the 55th FG's 45 Lightnings arrived to find the Liberators under attack by "a large force of 40 [sic] Me 110s as well as Me 109s and Fw 190s," but before they could intervene they were "bounced … by 30-plus single-engined fighters" – II./JG 11's Gustavs, the Zerstörers high cover – diving out of the sun from 33,000ft.

One P-38J was shot down – the pilot being killed – but Specht's unit lost three Me 109Gs, with two pilots killed and the third wounded.

Dispatched with 41 Mustangs, Colonel Henry Spicer's 357th FG had arrived earlier, but was plagued by a host of mechanical problems – engine troubles and running out of oxygen – reducing its strength considerably. Immediately after the bomb run, Spicer engaged the Zerstörers and damaged an Me 410 (claimed as a Ju 88 destroyed) and shot down an Me 110G over Erfurt. The rest of the 357th FG claimed four other "kills" but lost one 363rd FS P-51B, whose pilot was captured, to Fw 190As southwest of Eisenach at 1330hrs. Kogler's Zerstörers lost two Me 110Gs, with three crewmen killed.

There was a brief respite as, from 1318–1330hrs, 169 Liberators passed over their target, releasing 424 tons of bombs and incendiaries. Leading the first combat group, the 389th BG inadvertently dropped their ordnance on Eisenach. Wright Lee, a 445th BG bombardier, reported:

> The upcoming target was clear and easily identified. The Bf 110 [*sic*] factory buildings were snow covered but stood out clearly. I hit the salvo handle and away the bombs went at 1:19pm from 20,000 feet. I leaned down over the glass bottom of the nose and watched as our bombs fell toward the target. Then they hit the buildings which seemed to disintegrate and fly into the air. Black smoke and flames accompanied the explosions.

After delivering their bombloads, the column of Liberator formations made a sharp right turn, where the RLV interceptors "resumed their attacks with a vengeance," shooting down three more B-24Hs near Bad Hersfeld. Having shot down 22 B-24s, in exchange Graf's and Wilcke's units lost only one Focke-Wulf (I./JG 11) and two Gustavs (II./JG 3) – all three pilots being wounded – to the bombers' defensive fire.

The Liberators egressed to the east and were headed towards Koblenz when they were intercepted yet again. Having refueled at Rheine, ten JG 26 Fw 190As intercepted the 445th BG's ravaged and ragged formation near Giessen, north of Frankfurt, at 1355hrs. Oberleutnant Walter Matoni (5./JG 26) shot down one 702nd BS B-24H – hailed as JG 26's 2,000th victory of the war – followed quickly by a second one shot down by Leutnant Waldmar "Waldi" Radener, the 12-victory Staka of 7./JG 26. Twenty minutes later, near Asbach, Radener's Schwarm was attacked by a flight of 362nd FS P-51Bs which shot down and killed his wingman, but one Mustang developed engine trouble, forcing the pilot to bail out to become a POW. Meanwhile, 2. Staffel continued chasing the retiring Liberators, shooting down a 392nd BG B-24J northwest of Koblenz at 1410hrs.

Because Hodges' Liberators were the quickest to catch and the easiest to engage, they received almost all of I. Jagdkorps' attention. Over Germany, the 2nd Bombardment Division lost 27 B-24s to intercepting fighters, another (44th BG) to flak over the target, and one (93rd BG) to mechanical faults. During their return flight across Belgium, a navigation error resulted in Wood's 20th CBW straying over Brussels, where flak shot down two more Liberators (446th and 448th BGs). Additionally, a 389th BG B-24J, badly damaged by fighters in the target area,

Colonel Henry Spicer, the colorful and spirited 357th FG commander, in his P-51B-5 43-6880 "Tony Boy." His three victories were all scored during *Argument* escort missions. Within ten days, Spicer was shot down by flak to become a POW for the rest of the war. (USAF)

finally crashed near Malmedy in Belgium. Lastly, being too severely damaged to land, a 446th BG B-24H was abandoned over England.

This sacrifice gave Williams' 1st Bombardment Division a virtually free ride to Schweinfurt. After losing five Fortresses during their initial penetration, the long column of five combat wings turned south at Herford, where an early straggler was attacked by Oesau and his Stab flight, the JG 1 Kommodore shooting down a 92nd BG B-17 at 1240hrs, southeast of Hameln, for his 122nd victory.

Passing Bad Hersfeld, Williams' 238 bombers were joined by 25 Lightnings (20th FG) and eight Mustangs (354th FG) and entered Huth's 7. Jagddivision AOR (area of responsibility). Fortunately, Huth had launched all of his available day fighters, Zerstörers, Wild Sau, and twin-engine night-fighters and sent them south to intercept Twining's B-17s over Austria, so the only defenders in the area were Hackl's III./JG 11, originally part of Graf's Gefechtsverband. Taking off from Oldenburg at 1210hrs, while the rest of Graf's Jagdgeschwader was directed against Hodges' Liberators, Hackl's Jagdgruppe was vectored south to catch Williams' Fortresses. But catch them they could not; the long chase caused the Gustavs to run out of fuel and they wound up landing at airfields around Schweinfurt at 1325hrs, just as Turner's 40th CBW began their bomb runs.

Crossing the target unopposed – except by moderate flak – from 1327–1341hrs, the Flying Fortresses finally fulfilled the predictions of the pre-war air power prophets. Major George Shackley, leading the 381st BG, reported that "bombs were slamming down on factories and other targets in the city for at least a half an hour. Our own bombing was one of the best. This was one hell of a lot different from my first two Schweinfurt missions."

Over the target, three B-17Gs were damaged by flak, one (305th BG) crashing near Heilbronn as it attempted to limp to Switzerland. As it straggled homewards, another (303rd) was intercepted southwest of Koblenz by two Fw 190As (IV./JG 26) and shot down at 1410hrs. During the return flight, an Me 110G (9./ZG 26) attacked two formations at 23,000ft near Giessen, shooting down a 303rd BG B-17G southeast of the city at about 1350hrs and probably accounting for the 457th BG B-17G that crash-landed 12 miles to the north at 1345hrs. Immediately afterwards, the Zerstörer was shot down by a 20th FG P-38J, the aircrew bailing out safely.

About this time (1402hrs), the first "withdrawal support" P-47Ds – the 4th FG led by Lieutenant Colonel Selden Edner (former 336th FS CO, now 4th FG Operations Officer) – rendezvoused with the returning bombers near Koblenz, engaging several small formations without success, and lost one 335th FS Thunderbolt to a pair of IV./JG 26 Focke-Wulfs. It crashed southeast of Aachen at 1530hrs, killing the pilot.

As the returning American bombers once again approached the Dutch–German border at 1400hrs, Grabmann launched what little he had left – a handful of II. and III./JG 11 Schwärme – but they failed to score. The last Eighth AF loss of the day was at 1555hrs, when the 351st BG B-17G "Happy Warrior", which had been damaged by flak over Schweinfurt, was finally brought down 8 miles south of Amiens in northern France by a 7./JG 26 pilot, who was in turn shot down by the bomber's gunners. It was another successful – but very costly – victory by the Eighth AF.

The accurate and concentrated bombing of Schweinfurt's VKF factories caused major damage to three of them, with direct hits on machine shops, storage buildings, and power stations. The impact of this devastating daylight strike is difficult to ascertain because that night the RAF – 627 heavy bombers guided by the intense fires from the 1st Bombardment Division's 172 tons of incendiary bombs – added immeasurably to the wanton destruction.

Easier to measure were the effects of the Liberators' costly bombing of the Gotha Me 110 factory. While attacking at lower altitudes resulted in severe losses to RLV interceptors, it achieved its purpose; the "Bombing of Gotha was especially accurate." Post-strike assessment showed that almost a quarter – 93 bombs – of their payloads hit GWF factory buildings.

"Almost every building in the compact factory area was damaged. The eastern half of the plant, where aircraft manufacture [assembly] was centered, was generally destroyed," halting production for two weeks.

But the cost of success was high indeed. Hodges' 2nd Bomb Division lost 33 B-24s – over half from Timberlake's 2nd CBW – to enemy action, including three to flak, 13.8 percent of the strike force. Another 28 were damaged and a total of 327 aircrew were dead or missing. But Anderson's mission planning – sending in the Liberators first – and Schmid's concentration on the Gotha strike force resulted in Williams' 1st Bomb Division losing only 11 Fortresses – 4 percent of the strike force.

For the only time during Operation *Argument*, Schmid's command had attempted an all-out maximum effort. I. Jagdkorps launched elements of every Jagdgruppe on strength, totaling 336 sorties, but two of these units (III./JG 11 and III./JG 54) failed to intercept the American bombers on one of their missions. Luftflotte 3 launched an additional 143 sorties, but a quarter of these were transfer flights and ineffective missions (with no enemy encountered). About 450 sorties can be considered effective.

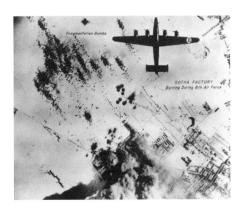

The 44th BG devastated the snow-covered Gotha Me 110G factory. At the factory airfield, 74 Me 110s were damaged or destroyed. (NMUSAF)

Schmid's assessment was that "all of our daytime fighter crews, despite the mental and physical stress caused by their almost steady commitment since the start of the American air offensive, fought stubbornly and courageously in the face of overwhelming American numerical superiority. Although their record of enemy aircraft destroyed was worthy of admiration, they were unable to prevent the American attack force from attaining its full effectiveness." In other words, despite the maximum effort, the day was a defeat for the Luftwaffe.

The OKL's Quartermaster recorded the loss of 60 aircraft written off the inventory of Luftflotte Reich and Luftflotte 3. More recent research shows that the actual losses (I. and II. Jagdkorps) totaled 53: 39 single-engine (21 Me 109Gs and 18 Fw 190As) day fighters, four Wild Sau night-fighters (one Me 109G and three Fw 190As), and three Zerstörers were lost, along with seven twin-engine night-fighters (six Me 110Gs and one Ju 88C). These losses represented 12.5 percent of the combat sorties launched. Losses in pilots were even more alarming – killed in action were 25 single-engine fighter pilots (including one Wild Sau pilot), along with three Zerstörer and ten night-fighter crewmen.

The Americans lost four escort fighters in air-to-air combat, plus three to mechanical failures and two to flak, with all nine pilots killed or captured. The lopsided air-to-air combat exchange ratio continued, with the day's score being 6.5:1 in the Americans' favor.

Eighth and Fifteenth AF Missions, February 25

The final mission of Operation *Argument* was planned to be the most concentrated attacks yet on German aviation industry targets. Over 900 bombers – from both the Eighth and Fifteenth AFs – would strike the heart of the Messerschmitt manufacturing facilities, located in Bavaria, with 50 more pursuing further destruction of anti-friction bearing production. The targets were the two Me 109G factories at Regensburg; the company's parent design, manufacturing, and testing facilities at Augsburg; the Flugzeugwerke Bachmann-von Blumenthal Me 110G factory at Fürth, a suburb of Nürnberg; and the SKF-Norma Compagnie GmbH roller-bearing plant at Cannstatt, the eastern suburb of Stuttgart. Because the forecast was for clear skies in the target areas, to ensure the best accuracy possible the mission would be flown at lower altitudes than usual.

Having suffered the least in the previous missions, LeMay's 3rd Bombardment Division was the strongest and would be leading the Eighth AF's 780 bombers on their flight deep into

Bavaria. Flying 570 miles from their bases in East Anglia, LeMay's five combat wings were planned to arrive over Regensburg about an hour after Twining's 150-strong strike force had hit the Prüfening component factory and turned for home, hopefully dragging Huth's interceptors southwards with them. Some 450 bombers were to attack the two Me 109G facilities.

Williams' 3rd Bomb Division – another 280 B-17s – would follow, with three combat wings striking the company's Augsburg facilities and the fourth hitting the SKF-Norma factory at Stuttgart. Finally, trailing the phalanx of Fortresses, Hodges' three combat wings – about 200 Liberators – were planned to bomb the Me 110G factory at Fürth.

This time – to use American sports analogies – Anderson's mission planners threw the German defenders a "curve ball." Instead of taking what the Jagdwaffe pilots called the "Bomber Autobahn" across northern Holland and the IJsselmeer – aiming directly at Berlin as if that were their destination – they planned an "end around" of 3. Jagddivision's AOR by initially flying south from England, crossing the Channel near Dieppe, then driving southeast across France to Sedan before turning east, crossing the Rhine near Landau, and fanning out across Bavaria to hit their four targets.

The 400-mile-long outflanking route stretched Kepner's VIII FC beyond its ability to maintain continuous fighter cover. Although Kepner provided 687 P-47Ds and Brigadier General Elwood R. Quesada's IX FC contributed 62 P-51Bs (363rd FG) for penetration and withdrawal support, since the initial thrust was through Oberst Carl Vieck's 4. Jagddivision AOR – which had only "Pips" Priller's JG 26 as its day-fighter force – at first the escort was thin; the primary penetration escort would join the bombers in the Sedan–Metz area. For "target area support" Kepner reserved 73 Lightnings and 77 Mustangs.

It was hoped that the initial advance by the main force would be aided by another North Sea diversion, this one being flown by the newly arrived 458th BG carrying APT-3 Mandrel noise jammers, just as the 92nd BG had on February 22 on their abortive and costly diversion to bomb Aalborg airfield. Instead of attempting to mask the assembly of the main strike group, the jammers would be providing enhanced radar returns on the Flugmeldedienst's EW radar frequencies and attempting to look like a much larger force than the 30-odd B-24s making up their formation.

B-17G-25-DL 42-38078 "Sweet Pea" of Fifteenth AF's 2nd BG, 429th BS, over the Alps. (USAF)

For once, the Eighth AF attack plan worked as designed. Beginning at 0900hrs, the Funkaufklärungsdienst informed Schmid and his I. Jagdkorps staff that large American formations were assembling over eastern England. Anticipating another deep strike into central Germany, Vieck dispatched Mietusch's III./JG 26 to Trier at 0940hrs to bolster Grabmann's depleted units, leaving him with only two Jagdgruppen. Two hours later – at 1109hrs – Flugmeldedienst's EW radars along the Dutch North Sea coast detected Colonel James Isbell's 458th BG 60 miles northwest of Vlieland island. The force was estimated "to consist of approximately 200 aircraft" headed northeast towards Denmark.

Only a minute later, Luftflotte 3 EW radar sites along the French Channel coast reported the approach of a second force, heading south from over Kent. As the minutes passed, the radar returns grew to represent "approximately 500 bombers." Crossing the French coast at Le Tréport, the giant stream of bombers turned southeast, heading towards Sedan.

Almost simultaneously, Twining's force – estimated at 200 bombers – was reported over Klagenfurt, headed northwest across Austria towards southeastern Germany.

Luftwaffe commands in Italy and Yugoslavia had actually been tracking the Fifteenth AF strike force for over an hour as 301 bombers flew up the Adriatic Sea towards Fiume. The leading formation was Lawrence's 5th BW, with 46 B-17s (2nd and 301st BGs) forming the main strike force with two other BGs (97th and 99th) planning to bomb storage facilities at Fiume and the Klagenfurt airfield along the way.

Following some way behind came Atkinson's 47th BW with 103 Liberators as the main group (449th, 450th, and 451st BGs), led by Colonel Robert Gideon, the 450th BG Deputy Commander. As a diversion, the 301st BW would be attacking Zara's (now Zadar in Croatia) port facilities and Fiume's railway yards. Later, Blanchard's 306th FW dispatched 85 Lightnings (1st and 14th FGs) for support in the target area and the initial withdrawal, with 40 P–47Ds (325th FG) rendezvousing in the Aviano–Udine area to escort the bombers home.

The bombers' route up the Adriatic and their initial lack of escorts signaled that they were on another deep penetration mission. Between 1005 and 1010hrs, Handrick launched Franzisket's I./JG 27, reinforced with a few Gustavs from the Verbändeführer Schule, and Michalski's II./JG 53, followed at 1100hrs by a training Jagdgruppe (I./JG 108) and Albrecht's II./ZG 1 Zerstörers. In a previously coordinated move, Handrik called for reinforcements from Oberstleutnant Günther Freiherr von Maltzahn's JaFü Oberitalien (Fighter Command Upper Italy), and between 1038 and 1040hrs I./JG 53 scrambled from Maniago and I./JG 77 from Lavariano, both bases between Aviano and Udine.

Approaching Fiume, Twining's two bomber formations "were pounced upon by more than 100 enemy fighters." Franzisket's I./JG 27 and Hauptmann Theo Lindemann's I./JG 77 concentrated on Lawrence's Fortresses – the main force now reduced to three dozen bombers due to air aborts, while 27 others sheared off to bomb Pola's warehouses – shooting down at least six B-17s from the 301st BG in a running battle all the way to Klagenfurt, as well as half a dozen more from the diversionary force. Meanwhile, Major Jürgen Harder's I./JG 53 and Michalski's II./JG 53 – totaling 35 Me 109Gs – attacked the 29 Liberators of 450th BG, leading Atkinson's strike force. Gideon's crews reported that "the enemy pilots were experienced and aggressive, employing every tactic in the book," quickly shooting down two B-24Hs before moving to attack the trailing 449th and 451st BGs, bringing down ten more. During the long running battle, the attacking Gustavs lost 14 aircraft – with two pilots killed and five wounded – to the bombers' defensive fire.

Meanwhile, from 1110–1130hrs Huth launched Dahl's III./JG 3, Gerlitz's I./JG 5, and Schroer's II./JG 27, reinforced by Brede's I./JG 301 Wild Sau, a fighter-training unit (I./JG 104), Kowalewski's ZG 76, a Zerstörer training unit (ZG 101), and a night-fighter training Gruppe (I./NJG 102). Since Doolittle's main strike force was just crossing the Channel into northeastern France at this time, Huth felt he had time to fly this maximum effort against Twining's bombers, now crossing Austria northwest of Klagenfurt heading towards Salzburg, and still recover, refuel, and rearm to meet the Eighth AF strike if they were going to attack targets within 7. Jagddivision's AOR.

The Fifteenth AF bombers reported "encountering up to 200 enemy fighters on the way to Regensburg which made well-coordinated [sic] attacks, using rockets, cannons and machine guns." Dahl's and Schroer's Jagdgruppen and I./ZG 76's Zerstörers concentrated against Lawrence's B-17s, shooting down another five from the 301st BG and three from the leading 2nd BG in the 90-minute air battle. Two of these were claimed by Schroer – at 1228 and 1231hrs over Chiemsee and Altötting – bringing his score to 98 victories.

Three Gustavs and five Me 110Gs were lost to the Fortresses' defensive fire, killing five aircrewmen and wounding five more. Gerlitz's I./JG 5 scrambled from Obertraubling just in time to intercept the bombers approaching Regensburg, but lost one Gustav shot down, its pilot being killed.

Werner Schroer became a Jagdwaffe pilot in August 1940, joining JG 27 at the height of the Battle of Britain. He was credited with 85 victories – including ten *Viermotoren* (four-motors) – in the Mediterranean theater and became commander of II./JG 27 in April 1943. Four months later, his Jagdgruppe was transferred to RLV duties, where he was credited with 11 more victories before Operation *Argument* began. (Author's Collection)

By the time Lawrence's badly depleted formation approached Prüfening, only two dozen Fortresses remained. Plowing through intense flak barrages, they "made a highly successful bomb run" at 1300hrs, fighter attacks continuing for 30 minutes afterwards. Following shortly behind, Gideon's B-24s waded "through intense and accurate flak, maintained a close formation, and scored many direct hits." But 22 of the 87 Liberators were damaged by flak – two of them crippled, both succumbing to the fighter attacks that continued for another 40 minutes. One of these was shot down by a II./JG 301 pilot at 1320hrs, but Brede's Stab flight lost one Me 109G-6, with the pilot wounded, to the arriving Lightnings. Homeward bound, Richard's 1st FG was "bounced" by Franzisket's I./JG 27 (on their second mission) and lost one P-38H shot down, another to mechanical (engine) failure, and a third written off upon return, with one pilot killed and another wounded.

Of 149 bombers dispatched against the main target, 111 bombed the Prüfening factory, losing 14 B-17s and 19 B-24s – 30 percent losses. Of the 124 bombers attacking diversionary targets, five Fortresses and one Liberator were lost. The Luftwaffe flew over 250 interceptor sorties but also lost heavily – 26 Me 109E/Gs and eight Me 110D/Gs, with five Jagdwaffe pilots and eight Zerstörer aircrew killed.

With no time to spare, Schröer's II./JG 27 landed at Schleißheim (near Munich) at 1250hrs, and 30 minutes later Dahl's III./JG 3 landed at Leipheim (near Ulm), both units being refueled and rearmed as quickly as possible so they could be launched against the Eighth AF B-17s that were already crossing the Rhine and heading towards Augsburg and Regensburg.

Two hours earlier, from 1110–1130hrs, Ninth AF Marauders struck 3. Jagddivision bases at Venlo in the Netherlands (IV./JG 3 – which was deployed to Volkel – and I./NJG 1) and Saint Trond in Belgium (II./NJG 1) to pave the way for Doolittle's heavy bombers. Thinking the B-26s were the first wave of Doolittle's main force, Borris' I./JG 26 was scrambled from Florennes between 1047 and 1051hrs and intercepted the 387th BG formation just off-shore. Before escorting RAF Typhoons could react, four 387th BG Marauders were shot down immediately, crashing into the sea at 1126hrs with the loss of all 27 aboard.

As the enormous American heavy bomber force – 558 B-17s and 196 B-24s – crossed the French Channel coast and turned towards Sedan, from 1100–1200hrs Generalmajor Karl Hentschel's 5. Jagddivision scrambled Major Egon Mayer's Stab/JG 2 from Cormeilles-en-Vexin and Bühlingen's II./JG 2 from Creil, along with a handful of Me 109Gs from a Jagdwaffe training unit (I./JG 101) based at Pou-Oest. Flying almost due east across northern France, Mayer's interceptors arrived in the area around Metz after the main air battles involving JG 26 units had occurred but were able to shoot down at least one straggler attempting to return to England.

With Vieck's deployment of JG 26's III. Gruppe to Trier and the despatch of I. Gruppe to intercept the Marauders, only Gäth's II. Gruppe remained, and it was down to 50 percent strength. As the bombers began streaming overhead Laon-Athies airfield at 1130hrs, Gäth launched a small formation led by 8./JG 26 Staka and nine-victory ace Hauptmann Rudolf Leuschel, ordering them to shadow the bomber stream and only attack unescorted Pulks. Also at 1130hrs, Grabmann scrambled Mietusch's III. Gruppe from Trier. Initially, the 20 Me 109Gs climbed to the east, then reversed course to intercept Williams' 1st Bombardment

Division near Charleville and Sedan at 1215hrs and quickly shot down two 306th BG Fortresses. Flak over Sedan brought down a 305th BG B-17G and damaged one from 457th BG so badly it fell out of formation and was shot down by fighters, crashing in the French Ardennes at 1230hrs.

Pursuing the bombers eastbound, past Saarbrücken, Hauptmann Hermann Staiger's 12./JG 26 shot down another 457th BG B-17G over Birkweiller at 1300hrs and damaged a third 306th BG Fortress so badly it crashed in a forest south of Karlsruhe. Mietusch's success would have continued had it not been for the arrival of Colonel Tom Christian's 361st FG, the Thunderbolts shooting down one Gustav without loss.

Leuschel's nine Fw 190As caught LeMay's 3rd Bombardment Division near Metz between 1200 and 1220hrs, their first frontal attack shooting down a 92nd BG B-17F. As Leuschel was reforming his flight, 4th FG Thunderbolts arrived and spotted Leuschel's Schwarm repositioning for a second pass. Captain Dominic "Don" Gentile led the 336th FS in a swooping attack that quickly shot down three of them.

In claiming his sixth victory, Gentile reported, "I closed to about 400 yards for my first burst. I opened fire again at 300 yards observing many strikes and large and small pieces coming off the '190. My whole aircraft was covered with oil, [and] my No. 2 man was hit by pieces of the enemy aircraft in the cowling and prop. When I last saw the '190, he was close to the ground going straight down." Leuschel and one wingman were shot down and killed, while another wingman bailed out unhurt. The fourth member of Leuschel's flight was later shot down while attempting to land at Saarbrücken airfield.

Approaching that city, flak was much more intense than anticipated and, flying at altitudes well within the lethal envelope of the highly effective 8.8cm flak guns, two 3rd Bomb Division Fortresses were shot down, one exploding in mid-air and the other crashing along the banks of the Saar River. Also damaged by both fighters and flak, a third attempted to return to base but was eventually shot down southeast of Laon at 1305hrs. Over Landau, a fourth Fortress was so badly damaged it turned south to escape to Switzerland, but was reported shot down by fighters near Stuttgart.

Meanwhile, at noon, Grabmann began launching Oesau's JG 1 from Rheine, Dortmund, and Volkel, reserving two Jagdgruppen (I. and IV./JG 3) to wait to see whether the "200 bombers" approaching Jutland or the "500 bombers" crossing western France was the primary threat.

The 4th FG's famous Lieutenant Don Gentile in the cockpit of his P-47. Having claimed two victories with RAF No. 133 Squadron, Gentile had added three Fw 190As to his score by the time *Argument* began. Once the former Eagle Squadron (336th FS) reequipped with P-51Bs, Gentile's scoring soared, shooting down 15 Luftwaffe aircraft (with one shared) and destroying six on the ground, becoming the first USAAF pilot to match Edward Rickenbacker's 26 victories in World War I. (USAF)

Twenty minutes later, Schmid's I. Jagdkorps staff finally realized that Isbell's 458th BG "was engaged in a diversionary maneuver. While still over the water, approximately 70 kilometers [43½ miles] west of the island of Sylt and Esbjerg [in Denmark] the American bombers reversed their course and headed back to Great Britain … [and] were last reported 100 kilometres [60 miles] west of [the] island of Terschelling at 1346hrs." The electronically enhanced diversionary force had exactly the desired effect: Ibel kept Graf's JG 11 interceptors on alert on the ground from 1100–1230hrs. By the time it was realized that the operation was a feint, Doolittle's main force was flying from Saarbrücken to Landau, driving eastwards beyond JG 11's ability to participate in the running battle across Bavaria.

Likewise, Lützow had kept III./JG 54 on the ground and instead launched I. and II./ZG 26 at 1230hrs in the hope that the longer-ranged Zerstörers could reach the American bomber stream in time. Ibel launched the last remnant of Kogler's III./ZG 26 at the same time. All that Huth had left were a few Me 110s from a night-fighter training unit, I./NJG 101, which was launched from Munich's Riem airfield against the bombers bound for Regensburg.

Oesau's JG 1 units headed southeast at high altitude and high speed. Such was the urgency that a proper Gefechtsverband could not be formed and the various formations were forced to engage individually. At 1305hrs, near Baden-Baden (south of Karlsruhe), Oesau claimed to have shot down a Fortress from an altitude of 21,325ft. Major Rudolf-Emil Schnoor's I. Gruppe intercepted Hodges' Fürth-bound 2nd Bombardment Division near Landau and shot down one 93rd BG B-24D at 1350hrs, although no victory was accredited. Hauptmann Friedrich Eberle's III. Gruppe intercepted the 45th CBW en route to Regensburg and shot down one 96th BG Fortress near Crailsheim at 1330hrs and damaged another so badly it attempted to escape to Switzerland, finally crashing 60 miles west-southwest of Regensburg. This B-17F may have become the victim of "Pritzl" Bär (6./JG 1), who claimed the "final destruction" (*endgültige Vernichtung*) of a Boeing near Stuttgart at 1343hrs.

Headed to Regensburg, LeMay's five combat wings were escorted by Colonel Bart Russell's 20th FG Lightnings and Spicer's 357th FG Mustangs. Russell's 29 P-38Js were not engaged, but a flight of 362nd FS P-51Bs spotted a solitary Me 109G about 2,000ft above the bombers and Captain Joe Broadhead climbed to attack. As he opened fire, "the Me 109 peeled off [and dived] into the bombers." As Broadhead and his wingman, Lieutenant Tom Beemer, dived through the bomber formation, Breemer's Mustang was hit by the Fortresses' .50-cal machine-gun fire, forcing him to bail out; he was badly injured when he hit the ground.

Meanwhile, Broadhead caught the Gustav, the Mustang pilot reporting that his adversary "saw me and made a quick bank to the left." He continued:

I closed fast to within 50 yards and observed strikes on his engine and right wing. He reversed direction and split-essed to the right. He then pulled out at 15,000ft, rolled twice to the left and began a shallow dive. I fired continuously, hitting him throughout the maneuver. As soon as he began his dive the aircraft started disintegrating. Cowling, canopy and various parts flew off.

Spicer's Mustangs claimed six victories, and I./JG 1 lost one Fw 190A before Oesau's units began returning to their bases to refuel and rearm. Meanwhile, launched from Volkel too late to get through the American escorts, I. and IV./JG 3 failed to score against the bombers, were engaged by Mustangs, and lost three Me 109Gs, with two pilots wounded. Huth's night-fighter training unit (I./NJG 101) was also engaged by the 362nd FS, losing three Me 110Gs; aircrew casualties are unknown.

Having lost only six B-17s to enemy action and with 17 others aborting the mission due to battle damage and mechanical problems, some 266 Fortresses arrived over Regensburg's Obertraubling and Prüfening factories between 1350 and 1409hrs, releasing 590 tons of bombs and incendiaries on their two targets with devastating accuracy.

Over Obertraubling, Wilson's 4th CBW waded through intense and accurate flak that shot down two 385th BG Fortresses. One crashed at the target; the other exploded in mid-air. Over Prüfening, flak knocked out one engine of a 100th BG B-17F – "Mismalovin" – which slowly fell out of formation after the bomb run and eventually straggled homewards by itself. Attacked repeatedly by fighters on the return flight, "Mismalovin" finally succumbed to its extensive battle damage, crashing into the sea off Calais, killing eight of the crew.

Escorting three 1st Bombardment Division combat wings to Augsburg were 44 P-38Hs from the 55th FG, but there was little opposition. Sweeping the route ahead, the 38th FS sighted a formation of ten Me 410s northeast of Ingolstadt. The P-38Hs dispersed the Hornissen, claiming one shot down (actually, none were lost). Meanwhile, attacking from astern, ZG 26's Me 110Gs damaged a 92nd BG B-17F so badly that the crew headed for Switzerland, crash-landing at Dubendorf at 1518hrs.

After losing nine B-17s to enemy action and having 13 others turn back with battle damage or various problems, from 1352–1415hrs 165 Fortresses dropped approximately 271.5 tons of bombs on the large

Following great success in the Battle of Britain (46 victories) and Operation *Barbarossa* (44 victories), Walter "Gulle" Oesau commanded JG 2 Richthofen Geschwader in France and then the RLV's JG 1, where he became an *experte* at shooting down Viermotoren (four-engines), claiming 14 victories over B-17s and B-24s. Following his death on May 11, 1944, JG 1 was titled the Oesau Geschwader. (Author's Collection)

Messerschmitt facilities. The 381st BG's lead bombardier, Lieutenant Happy Hendryx, reported, "Bombing was very good. We knocked out at least three-quarters of the factory. We had a good formation and made an ideal bomb run, laying our bombs in a tight pattern. All we could see was smoke when we turned to head back."

Guided to Stuttgart by the column of smoke from fires still burning from the RAF's raid four nights previously, 50 Fortresses dropped 168 tons of bombs on the SKF-Norma roller-bearing factory. The only threat was flak – the 303rd BG had 23 out of 25 bombers damaged by it.

With the Fortresses ahead attracting almost all of the Luftwaffe's attentions, Hodges' Liberators had a virtual free ride to Fürth, losing only one bomber to enemy action while 15 others aborted due to mechanical and other problems. From 1402–1420hrs, 172 B-24s delivered 395 tons of bombs on the Bachmann-von Blumenthal Me 110G factory with excellent accuracy. Releasing their bombloads from 18,000ft, the attackers lost two Liberators to the local flak batteries.

As 1,425 tons of bombs rained down upon their targets, Huth launched his second wave of interceptors around 1400hrs: Dahl's III./JG 3 from Leipheim, Schroer's II./JG 27 from Schleißheim, and Kowalewski's ZG 76, augmented by Zerstörer and Jagdwaffe training units (I./ZG 101 and I./JG 106). Dahl's formation caught Gross's 1st CBW formation as they headed home from Augsburg, damaging a 381st BG B-17G so badly that it eventually crashed near Reutlingen at 1445hrs. Lieutenant Don Henderson and his crew were flying their 25th and final mission – only four crewmen managed to bail out and survive.

Huth's interceptors were countered by Spicer's Mustangs, which swept southeast along the Danube to Ulm, the 362nd FG engaging Dahl's III./JG 3 and shooting down two Me 109Gs – both pilots being killed – for the loss of one P-51B, its pilot bailing out to become a POW. Schroer's II./JG 27 lost one Gustav, its pilot being wounded.

Meanwhile, from 1415–1420hrs, Grabmann launched Oesau's Stab and II./JG 1 to intercept the egressing bombers, and scrambled Mietusch's III./JG 26 from Trier at 1430hrs, which was joined by "Waldi" Radener's 7. Staffel – five Fw 190As that had launched from Cambrai-Epinoy at 1352hrs.

By this time, "Big Jim" Howard's 354th FG Mustangs – who claimed to shoot down a total of seven German fighters during the mission to Fürth – had already departed for England, low on fuel, and the first "withdrawal support units" had yet to arrive, making the returning bombers very vulnerable, especially the stragglers. At 1500hrs, "Gulle" Oesau attacked a lone 445th BG B-24H at 16,400ft near Baden-Baden, claiming it as his 124th victory. Seegatz's II./JG 1 intercepted Hodges' returning Liberators near Karlsruhe, where flak had damaged several, creating more stragglers. "Pritzl" Bär and his wingman attacked one of these – a 93rd BG B-24J – over the Rhine east of Landau at 1455hrs; it became Bär's 191st credited victory.

Three B-17s were also lost in the Pirmasens area, apparently all to JG 26 interceptors. Radener and his small Staffel shot down a 305th BG B-17G that crashed at Zweibrücken at 1515hrs. Although claimed as Herausschüssen, the 379th and 447th BG's losses were probably the victims of Mietusch – his 58th victory – and 9./JG 26 Staka 18-victory ace Oberleutnant Hans-Georg Dippel. Attempting to catch the last few stragglers, Hentschel launched III./JG 2 from Cormeilles-en-Vexin, which claimed one B-17 destroyed – probably the 96th BG B-17G that crashed near Rethel in the French Ardennes at 1610hrs.

The day's final bomber losses were "The Lady from Bristol," a 448th BG B-24H that became a straggler and crashed into the sea, another 448th Liberator that crashed at Chipping Ongar in Essex due to fuel exhaustion and "Mr Terrific," a 447th BG B-17G that was abandoned over England. Additionally, one Fortress (457th BG) and two Liberators (44th and 392nd BGs) were written off as salvage.

At the cost of 34 bombers – with 301 men missing, four killed, and 26 wounded – Doolittle's Eighth AF had scored a great victory.

Having been a primary target for two of the six days of "Big Week," by the end of the campaign, Messerschmitt's Regensburg facilities were devastated. Lost production totaled 300 fighters, and the two factories did not return to planned production levels for four months. At Augsburg, 30 buildings were destroyed, along with 30 percent of the machine tools and 70 percent of stored materials, reducing production to 35 percent for the next month. Even Schmid acknowledged, "All the aircraft factories attacked on 25 February suffered heavy damages."

Against the 903 American bombers entering Nazi airspace, the Luftwaffe had flown 490 sorties, over half of these against the Fifteenth AF's 149 bombers. Against Doolittle's 754 bombers, Schmid's I. Jagdkorps (1., 2., and 3. Jagddivisionen) launched only 100 interceptors, the remaining sorties being flown by Luftflotten 2 and 3. Of the 100 RLV sorties launched, Schmid lost 24 fighters destroyed or written off, with four pilots killed and eight wounded. Escorting Eighth and Ninth AF fighters accounted for 16 of these (seven Me 109Gs, five Fw 190As, and four Me 110s), for the loss of only one Mustang to enemy action.

The reason that Schmid was able to meet the deep penetrations into Bavaria with only half his forces was, in his words, proof that "the American diversionary maneuver over the North Sea may be considered a success," pinning five Jagdgruppen (all of JG 11, II./JG 3, and III./JG 54) to the ground in northern Germany. The five Jagdgruppen with which he responded (all of JG 1, and I. and IV./JG 3) were unable to organize any effective Gefechtsverbände and were forced to fight in Staffel-size formations that had to resort to picking off stragglers rather than seriously attriting any of Doolittle's four strike forces.

Of the 26 American bombers lost to enemy action over German-held territory, the paucity of RLV interceptors resulted in only 14 being shot down solely by them. Six others were brought down due to flak and another half dozen were picked off as stragglers after being damaged by flak. The lack of attrition of the bomber forces made their attacks all the more effective, resulting in greater destruction to the four targets.

In his report, Schmid acknowledged, "All things considered, 25 February must be chalked up as a failure for I. Jagdkorps."

AFTERMATH AND ASSESSMENT

The scale of this offensive, the care with which it was planned, the precision with which it was executed, and the success which it achieved should establish it for all time as a landmark in the history of aerial warfare.

Combined Operational Planning Committee, Report on Operation *Argument*,
June 23, 1944

Operation *Argument* ended just as it began, with an RAF Bomber Command air raid. This one, guided by the fires that still raged at and around the Augsburg Messerschmitt works, consisted of 594 Mosquitos and heavy bombers that released their bombloads from 2105–2132hrs that night. Sixteen Lancasters, five Halifaxes, and a Mosquito (four of these due to collision) lost over German territory that night in exchange for killing 730 civilians and, because frozen hydrants and water surfaces prevented effective fire-fighting, causing 246 fires that destroyed the city center and a quarter of the homes, leaving 85,000 homeless.

Atrocious northern European winter weather then closed in, precluding any further bombing missions, and Operation *Argument* was over. All campaigns, except the one that achieves final victory, have a sequel, and this one's sequel was Eighth AF's Battle of Berlin, begun on March 6 following a largely aborted initial attempt two days before.

While the target was different, the aim was the same – get the Luftwaffe to launch as many interceptors as possible so they could be destroyed by American fighters. By March 8, Kepner had four P-51B FGs, plus Quesada's two, providing heavy escort in the target area. Berlin was effectively attacked four times in March, resulting in 157 interceptors destroyed or written off, for the loss of 65 escorting fighters.

Having done what it could to reduce the Luftwaffe's strength, the Eighth AF was attached to Eisenhower's command on April 1 for Operation *Overlord* and began a campaign intended to limit the Wehrmacht's ability to shift forces into and across France to meet the Normandy invasion.

But how effective had *Argument* been?

The men largely responsible for the success of Operation *Argument* – Major General William Kepner (sitting, center) and his VIII FC fighter group commanders. These great leaders included Colonel Hubert Zemke (56th FG, rear, far left), Lieutenant Colonel Donald Blakeslee (4th FG, rear, second from the left), and Lieutenant Colonel Glenn E. Duncan (353rd FG, middle row, third from left). (NARA Ref 342-FH-3A47576-55088AC)

Of the original 16 aircraft industry targets, 1,880 American bomber sorties hit 11 of them with over 5,000 tons of bombs. Of these, six were so badly damaged that fighter production was temporarily reduced to less than half of that planned. Instead of manufacturing 2,000 single-engine fighters a month, RLM figures totaled 926 produced in February and 900 in March, a shortfall of 2,174 interceptors (not counting dedicated ground-attack and reconnaissance versions) in the six weeks following the campaign. Instead of 500 twin-engine Zerstörers and night-fighters, in these two months only 351 Me 110s/410s were made, a shortfall of 149 aircraft.

In a meeting to assess the campaign's impact on the Nazi aircraft industry, Milch confessed, "The effect on our day fighter production has been very severe and we are faced with difficulties… But the struggle is not hopeless, it can be managed. We should reach a monthly output of 2,000 fighters by the end of February." Single-engine fighter production did not meet Milch's goal until June – and by then it was too late.

While Milch's optimistic forecast was off by four months, the rapid recovery of the German aircraft industry to the point of producing an average of 1,523 fighters monthly by July proved surprising to USSTAF staffs. It has also frequently been cited by amateur historians and Luftwaffe enthusiasts as evidence that *Argument* failed to achieve its aim. But they miss the point.

Operation *Argument* was not so much about bombing the Nazi aircraft factories as it was about destroying the Luftwaffe in the air, just as Doolittle had stated that "the first duty of Eighth Air Force fighters is to destroy German fighters" – and this they did well.

In six days of combat, the OKL Quartermaster registered 282 losses in the West and over the Reich. More accurately, Caldwell's exhaustive research – including Austrian and Italian-based units – tallied 294 destroyed: 238 single-engine interceptors and 58 Zerstörers (178 Me 109Gs, 60 FW 190As, 52 Me 110Gs, and four Me 410s) plus two Me 110 "shadowers". While February's markedly reduced fighter production – 825 Gustavs, 101 Focke-Wulfs, and 125 Zerstörers – could replace these losses, it was the fighter pilot and aircrew losses that were the critical factor. Eighty-eight Jagdwaffe and Wild Sau pilots and 63 Zerstörer crewmen had been killed. These could not be immediately replaced because, due to the terrible winter weather, the Luftwaffe's training programs graduated no replacements until mid-March 1944.

The effect of the unrelenting attrition during *Argument* showed itself in the steady deterioration of the RLV's ability to combat American operations. "Big Week" began with regularly organized Gefechtsverbände of two or three Jagdgruppen (about 60 fighters) making massed frontal attacks against the American bomber wings. By the end of the week, units were so depleted that they could rarely organize anything larger than Staffel-size formations that were limited to making hit-and-run attacks and picking off individual stragglers. The front-line units were so badly depleted that training units had to be launched to augment operational ones.

The victory by Kepner's VIII FC – which lost 15 fighters (seven P-51Bs, seven P-47Ds, and one P-38J) in air-to-air combat out of 31 lost overall – came at the cost of 226 bombers. For two of the six days, Anderson's mission planners were able to use misdirection, circuitous routing, and electronic means to fool Schmid's controllers, keeping several Jagdgruppen from joining the battle, thus limiting the numbers of RLV interceptors engaged and providing Kepner's fighter pilots with numerical superiority in most fighter-vs-fighter battles.

On the other days, weather and timing errors denied some bomber formations their fighter protection, resulting in serious losses. Doolittle's Eighth AF flew a total of 3,328 effective sorties and lost 137 bombers, a 4.11 percent loss rate. Twining's Fifteenth AF flew 549 largely unescorted sorties and lost 89 bombers, a 16.2 percent loss rate. Clearly, fighter escorts made a substantial and dramatic difference.

As their contribution to *Argument*, RAF Bomber Command flew 2,351 sorties, dropping 9,198 (US) tons of bombs on Leipzig, Stuttgart, Schweinfurt, Steyr, and Augsburg, losing 157 bombers, a loss rate of 6.6 percent. At this point, escorted daylight attacks – which were more accurate and far more destructive against specific targets – had become less costly than night-bombing.

By the end of *Argument*, Schmid admitted that the Luftwaffe's final defeat had begun, confessing, "In numbers as well as in technical performance, the daytime fighter units assigned to German air defense activity are inferior to American fighter aircraft forces. In spite of their demonstrated willingness to make every sacrifice for their country, in the long run our forces are fighting a hopeless battle."

BIBLIOGRAPHY

Berenbrok, Hans-Dieter (writing as Cajus Bekker), *The Luftwaffe War Diaries: The German Air Force in World War II*, Doubleday & Company, New York (1968).

Bishop, Stan D. & Hey, John A., *Losses of the US 8th and 9th Air Forces, Volume 2 ETO Area January 1944 – March 1944*, Bishop Book Productions, Yeovil, UK (2007).

Boatner, Mark M. III, *The Biographical Dictionary of World War II*, Presidio Press, Novato, CA (1996).

Bucholtz, Chris, *Osprey Aircraft of the Aces 96: Mustang Aces of the 357th Fighter Group*, Osprey Publishing Limited, Oxford (2010).

Bucholtz, Chris, *Osprey Aviation Elite Units 30: 4th Fighter Group 'Debden Eagles'*, Osprey Publishing Limited, Oxford (2008).

Caldwell, Donald, *Day Fighters in Defence of the Reich, A War Diary, 1942–1945*, Frontline Books, Pen & Sword Books Ltd, Barnsley, UK (2011).

Caldwell, Donald, *The JG 26 War Diary, Volume Two 1943–1945*, Grub Street, London (1998).

Caldwell, Donald & Muller, Richard, *The Luftwaffe over Germany: Defence of the Reich*, Frontline Books, Pen & Sword Books Ltd, Barnsley, UK (2014).

Cleaver, Thomas McKelvey, *Osprey Aircraft of the Aces 115: Aces of the 78th Fighter Group*, Osprey Publishing Limited, Oxford (2013).

Cooper, Alan, *Target Leipzig: The RAF's Disastrous Raid of 19/20 February 1944*, Pen & Sword Aviation (2009).

Copp, DeWitt S., *A Few Great Captains: The Men and Events that Shaped the Development of U.S. Air Power*, Doubleday & Company, Inc., Garden City, NY (1980).

Copp, DeWitt S., *Forged in Fire: Strategy and Decisions in the Airwar over Europe 1940–1945*, Doubleday & Company, Inc., Garden City, NY (1982).

Ferguson, Arthur B., *The Army Air Forces in World War II, Volume Three, Europe: Argument to V-E Day, January 1944 to May 1945*, edited by Wesley Frank Craven and James Lea Cate, Office of Air Force History, Washington, DC (1983, reprint of 1949 edition).

Forsyth, Robert, *Osprey Aircraft of the Aces 101: Luftwaffe Viermot Aces, 1942–45*, Osprey Publishing Limited, Oxford (2011).

Forsyth, Robert, *Osprey Combat Aircraft 131: Me 210/410 Zerstörer Units*, Osprey Publishing Limited, Oxford (2019).

Freeman, Roger A., *The Mighty Eighth: A History of the U.S. 8th Army Air Force*, Doubleday and Company, Inc., Garden City, NY (1970).

Freeman, Roger A., *Zemke's Wolfpack: The Story of Hub Zemke and the 56th Fighter Group in the Skies over Europe*, Orion Books, NY (1988).

Freeman, Roger A. with Crouchman, Alan & Maslen, Vic, *The Mighty Eighth War Diary*, Motorbooks International, Fry (1981).

Gabrieski, Francis, *Gabby: A Fighter Pilot's Life*, Orion Books, NY (1991).

Garry L. & Ethell, Jeffrey L., *Escort to Berlin*, Arco Publishing, Inc., NY (1980).

Gray, John M., *The 55th Fighter Group vs The Luftwaffe*, Specialty Press Publishers, North Branch, MN (1998).

Hess, William N., *Osprey Aviation Elite 7: 354th Fighter Group*, Osprey Publishing Limited, Oxford (2002).

Hess, William N. & Ivie, Thomas G., *Fighters of the Mighty Eighth 1942–1945*, Motorbooks International, Osceola, WI (1990).

Ivie, Thomas G., *Osprey Aviation Elite 8: 352nd Fighter Group*, Osprey Publishing Limited, Oxford (2002).

Lorant, Jean-Yves & Goyat, Richard, *Jagdgeschwader 300 'Wild Sau': A Chronicle of a Fighter Geschwader in the Battle for Germany*, Eagle Editions Ltd, Hamilton, MT (2005).

Marshall, Francis L., *Sea Eagles: The Messerschmitt Bf 109T, 1942–1944*, Air Research Publications, Walton on Thames, UK (1993).

McFarland, Stephen L. & Newton, Wesley Phillips, *To Command the Sky: The Battle for Air Superiority over Germany, 1942–1944*, Smithsonian Institution Press, Washington, DC (1991).

MacKay, Ron, *20th Fighter Group*, Squadron/Signal Publications, Inc., Carrollton, TX (1995).

MacKay, Ron, *381st Bomb Group*, Squadron/Signal Publications, Inc, Carrollton, TX (1995).

Mullins, John D., *An Escort of P-38s: The 1st Fighter Group in World War II*, Phalanx Publishing Co., Ltd, St Paul, MN (1995).

Olmsted, Merle, *The 357th Over Europe: The 357th Fighter Group in World War II*, Phalanx Publishing Co., Ltd, St Paul, MN (1994).

Price, Alfred, *The Luftwaffe Data Book*, Greenhill Books, London (1997).

Reschke, Willi, *Jagdgeschwader 301/302 'Wild Sau': In Defense of the Reich with the Bf 109, FW 190, and Ta 152*, Schiffer Publishing, Ltd, Atglen, PA (2005).

Rust, Kenn C., *Fifteenth Air Force Story in World War II*, Sunshine House, Inc., Terre Haute, IN (1976).

Rust, Kenn C., *The 9th Air Force in World War II: from the Desert to Central Germany*, Aero Publishers, Inc., Fallbrook, CA (1967).

Schmid, Josef, Generalleutnant (Ret.), 'The Employment of the German Luftwaffe against the Allies in the West 1943–1945, Volume II: The Struggle for Air Superiority over the Reich, 1 January 1944 – 31 March 1944', unpublished USAF Historical Study No. 159 (Göggingen, Germany, 1954) on file at USAF Historical Research Agency, Maxwell AFB, AL.

Smith, Jack H., *Osprey Aviation Elite Units 10: 359th Fighter Group*, Osprey Publishing Limited, Oxford (2002).

Weal, John, *Osprey Aircraft of the Aces 25: Messerschmitt Bf 110 Zerstörer Aces of World War 2*, Osprey Publishing Limited, Oxford (1999).

Weal, John, *Osprey Aircraft of the Aces 68: Bf 109 Defence of the Reich Aces*, Osprey Publishing Limited, Oxford (2006).

Weal, John, *Osprey Aircraft of the Aces 92: Fw 190 Defence of the Reich Aces*, Osprey Publishing Limited, Oxford (2011).

Weal, John, *Osprey Aircraft of the Aces 116: Aces of Jagdgeschwader 3 'Udet'*, Osprey Publishing Limited, Oxford (2013).

Weal, John, *Osprey Aviation Elite Units 20: Luftwaffe Sturmgruppen*, Osprey Publishing Limited, Oxford (2005).

Yenne, Bill, *Big Week: Six Days That Changed the Course of World War II*, Berkley Publishing, NY (2013).

Zaloga, Steven J., *Osprey Fortress 107: Defence of the Third Reich 1941–45*, Osprey Publishing Limited, Oxford (2012).

INDEX